Abnormal Psychology

Abnormal Psychology

FOURTH EDITION

Martin E. P. Seligman
Elaine F. Walker
David L. Rosenhan

Bradley T. Connor
UNIVERSITY OF CALIFORNIA, LOS ANGELES

 W • W • NORTON & COMPANY • NEW YORK • LONDON

ISBN 0-393-97731-5 (pbk.)

W. W. Norton & Company, Inc., 500 Fifth Avenue, New York, NY 10110
www.wwnorton.com

W. W. Norton & Company Ltd., Castle House, 75/76 Wells Street, London W1T 3QT

1 2 3 4 5 6 7 8 9 0

CONTENTS

Preface

Testing students in lecture hall or classroom is often a daunting task fraught with pitfalls. While no testing method is without its controversies, multiple-choice tests are among the best ways of gauging a student's acquired knowledge over a semester or quarter, especially in courses with a large number of students. This test bank is provided as a tool for professors to use in assessing student mastery and in determining the effectiveness of their own teaching practices.

Included in this test bank are many new items as well as many items that have been adapted and revised from the third edition, developed by Lisa Butler. The items for this test bank have been written and revised (with answers and page references provided for each question) with certain issues and principles in mind. Among these issues is the need for clear and distinct answer choices. Ambiguous answers, or multiple answers that could suffice as the correct answer, can create havoc for students and professors. Care has therefore been taken to provide five distinct choices for each question. Sometimes included among these five choices are "all of the above" and "none of the above," as well as multiple-answer choices (e.g., "a and b only"). While these answers are often found to make test items more difficult, they also provide a method for testing a student's ability to integrate knowledge and combine information from different topic areas. As with any forced-choice test, it is always important to instruct students to choose the best possible answer and to read each question and each possible answer carefully. Additionally, in this edition attempts have been made to provide different formats, including applied formats, for tapping the same knowledge. So when selecting items from the test bank, it is important that teachers read each item carefully to ensure that differently formatted items tapping the same information are not included in the same exam. With these issues in mind, test construction using this test bank should be eased.

CHAPTER 1 | Abnormality: Past and Present

1. As of 1999, the surgeon general of the United States reported that
   a. 20 percent of all Americans suffer from mental illness in any given year.
   b. 40 percent of all Americans suffer from mental illness in any given year.
   c. the worldwide prevalence of mental illness is above 30 percent.
   d. the prevalence of mental illness in the United States is approximately 35 percent at any given time.
   e. the number of cases of reported mental illness was significantly declining.

   Answer: a   p. 4

2. If you were a believer of the top-down approach as described in the text, it is likely that you would believe
   a. that biological processes create mental processes.
   b. that biological states create mental states.
   c. that psychological states create biological states.
   d. that psychological processes create biological processes.
   e. none of the above.

   Answer: c   p. 6

3. The text emphasizes four themes important to abnormal psychology. Which of the following is *not* one of those themes?
   a. Biological versus psychological
   b. Cognitive versus psychoanalytic
   c. Science and practice
   d. Treatment of choice
   e. Development

   Answer: b   p. 7

4. The primary difference between efficacy studies and effectiveness studies is
    a. that efficacy studies are completed in the laboratory and effectiveness studies are conducted in the real world.
    b. that efficacy studies are outcome studies while effectiveness studies are evaluation studies.
    c. that effectiveness studies are conducted in the laboratory and efficacy studies are conducted in the real world.
    d. that effectiveness studies are for testing drugs and efficacy studies are for testing different types of therapies.
    e. none of the above.

    Answer: a   p. 11

5. In the animistic era, abnormality was commonly attributed to
    a. alcoholism.
    b. holes in the skull.
    c. physical Illness.
    d. opiate addiction.
    e. possession by spirits.

    Answer: e   p. 12

6. The practice whereby evil spirits are believed to be released through holes in the skull is called
    a. lobotomy.
    b. exorcism.
    c. purging.
    d. trephining.
    e. siphoning.

    Answer: d   p. 12

7. If you had the misfortune to be on trial in Salem for witchcraft, which of the following criteria would you most wish to have applied to test your innocence?
    a. Weak tests of witchcraft
    b. Strong tests of witchcraft
    c. Confession
    d. The testimony of others
    e. Presence of improbable facts

    Answer: b   p. 13

8. In retrospect, we can recognize that the widespread fear of witches involved fear of
   a. God's will.
   b. men's brutality.
   c. people's inhumanity.
   d. the unknown.
   e. women's sexuality.

   Answer: e   p. 13

9. One of the first psychological disorders thought to have arisen from physical causes was
   a. schizophrenia.
   b. depression.
   c. possession.
   d. hysteria.
   e. mania.

   Answer: d   p. 14

10. When first described by the Greeks, hysteria was attributed to
    a. chronic masturbation.
    b. idle thoughts.
    c. impure blood.
    d. an overactive liver.
    e. a wandering uterus.

    Answer: e   p. 14

11. The doctrine of animalism holds
    a. that people who are mad are very similar to animals.
    b. that people who are mad are prone to violence and so are animals.
    c. that animals live in miserable conditions without protest and so can the mad.
    d. all of the above.
    e. a and c.

    Answer: d   p. 14

12. The doctrine of animalism gave reason for the mad to be housed in miserable conditions until the late the eighteenth century because it stated that
    a. this was the best way to help the insane.
    b. this was the best way to punish insane.
    c. these were the only accommodations available.
    d. it made no difference to the insane how they were kept, as they did not protest.
    e. this was how the insane preferred to live.

    Answer: d   p. 15

13. Galen was one of the first to believe that
    a. physical pain could cause psychological distress.
    b. physical disorders could have psychological causes.
    c. psychological disorders could have physical causes.
    d. physical pain was caused by a wandering uterus.
    e. psychological disorders were caused by a wandering uterus.

    Answer: b   p. 15

14. The person who brought psychological causes back into the explanation of abnormality was
    a. Breuer.
    b. Charcot.
    c. Freud.
    d. Kraepelin.
    e. Mesmer.

    Answer: e   p. 16

15. Mesmer believed that many mental diseases developed from
    a. pyschogenic causes.
    b. animal-like urges and desires.
    c. obstruction of animal magnetism.
    d. hyperactive animal magnetism.
    e. physical causes.

    Answer: c   p. 16

16. Mesmer was accused of being a genius and a charlatan at the same time and was likely influenced by
    a. technological advances taking places during the time.
    b. great thinkers like Galen who came before him.
    c. his mentor, Charcot.
    d. opiate addiction.
    e. the great psychological minds in Vienna at the time.

    Answer: a   p. 16

17. The Royal Commission that investigated Mesmer disputed his
    a. cures.
    b. rationales.
    c. techniques.
    d. suggestions.
    e. hypotheses involving lunar cycles.

    Answer: b   p. 16

18. Facets of Mesmerism continue to exist in today's psychology as
    a. behavior modification.
    b. gestalt therapy.
    c. psychoanalysis.
    d. hypnotism.
    e. scientology.

    Answer: d   p. 16

19. Charcot used hypnosis for the purpose of
    a. distinguishing between convulsions caused by hysteria and those caused by epilepsy.
    b. distinguishing between mental illness and physical illness.
    c. recovering lost memories in his patients.
    d. removing psychological pain in his patients.
    e. none of the above.

    Answer: a   p. 16

20. A frequent experience that Charcot's patients had while under hypnosis was
    a. regression.
    b. catharsis.
    c. emotional reexperience.
    d. remembrance of lost memories.
    e. reliving the Oedipal complex.

    Answer: b   p. 17

21. One of Charcot's students was
    a. Galen.
    b. Skinner.
    c. Freud.
    d. Mesmer.
    e. none of the above.

    Answer: c   p. 17

22. Psychiatric hospitals began as shelters and prisons for
    a. the homeless.
    b. the poor.
    c. the insane.
    d. all of the above.
    e. a and c.

    Answer: d   p. 18

23. The original concern motivating the creation and maintenance of hospitals was
    a. medical.
    b. moral.
    c. psychological/psychiatric.
    d. political.
    e. religious.

    Answer: b   p. 18

24. Early treatments for the mentally ill, often described as cruel and punishing, grew out of
    a. religious theology.
    b. poorly trained psychologists/psychiatrists.
    c. experimental science.
    d. prevailing theories of the time.
    e. sadistic physicians.

    Answer: d   p. 18

25. One of the ways that the definition of abnormality differs is
    a. across cultures.
    b. across time.
    c. It does not differ.
    d. a and b.
    e. none of the above.

    Answer: d   p. 20

26. Which of the following is *not* considered one of the seven elements of abnormality?
    a. Suffering
    b. Maladaptiveness
    c. Social definitions
    d. Irrationality
    e. Loss of control

    Answer: c   p. 20

27. Which of the following involves the failure to achieve one's goals?
    a. Suffering
    b. Maladaptiveness
    c. Irrationality
    d. Unpredictability
    e. Unconventonality

    Answer: b   p. 21

28. A patient comes to see you complaining that his life has lost all meaning and he sees no reason to go on living. You learn that he has not suffered any recent losses, nor are there any serious problems in his work or social relationships. You begin to consider that his condition may be abnormal on the basis of which of the following criteria?
    a. Irrationality.
    b. Suffering.
    c. Observer discomfort.
    d. Maladaptiveness.
    e. Violation of standards.

    Answer: b   p. 21

29. According to the text, behavior may be judged to be out of control when
    a. an individual does not know the source of her actions.
    b. ordinary guidelines of behavior suddenly break down.
    c. ordinary inhibitors of behavior break down.
    d. ordinary inhibitors of behavior suddenly break down.
    e. all of the above.

    Answer: e   p. 22

30. The DSM-IV uses an approach to recognizing abnormality based on
    a. family resemblances.
    b. religious teachings.
    c. society mores.
    d. psychodynamic perspectives.
    e. empirical data.

    Answer: b   p. 23

31. Employing the family resemblance approach, a good example of abnormality is
    a. simple phobia.
    b. obsessive-compulsive disorder.
    c. schizophrenia.
    d. sexual fetishes.
    e. mania.

    Answer: c   p. 24

32. Intern's Syndrome is likely caused by
    a. family resemblances.
    b. the power of suggestion.
    c. stress.
    d. abnormality.
    e. unresolved conflicts.

    Answer: b   p. 26

33. The most important way to discover the cause of abnormality may be
    a. choosing a theoretical orientation and sticking to it.
    b. exploring diseases one by one to understand their causes.
    c. using an eclectic approach that includes the biological and psychological perspectives.
    d. using a top-down approach.
    e. using a bottom-up approach.

    Answer: c   p. 28

CHAPTER 2 | Assessment, Diagnosis, and Research Methods

1. A psychological assessment is an evaluation of a person's
   a. health.
   b. mental functioning and psychological health.
   c. level of sanity.
   d. psychological diagnosis.
   e. all of the above.

   Answer: b   p. 33

2. Psychological assessment of an individual may yield
   a. a diagnosis.
   b. an understanding of the client's individuality.
   c. an understanding of the difficulty facing the client.
   d. clues about how the difficulty can be resolved.
   e. all of the above.

   Answer: e   p. 34

3. If your thermometer gives you the same reading five minutes apart, you could say that it is
   a. valid.
   b. calibrated.
   c. reliable.
   d. standardized.
   e. a and b.

   Answer: c   p. 34

4. A rubber yardstick is
   a. reliable.
   b. invalid.
   c. unreliable.
   d. not standardized.
   e. b and c.

   Answer: c   p. 34

5. If you are taking an intelligence test and it reveals that you are good at sports, you could say that the intelligence test is
   a. valid.
   b. not reliable.
   c. not standardized.
   d. not valid.
   e. b and d.

   Answer: d   p. 34

6. The three general categories of psychological assessment are
   a. interviewing, observing, and testing.
   b. interviewing, assessing, and diagnosing.
   c. assessing, diagnosing, and theorizing a treatment.
   d. interviewing, diagnosing, and developing a treatment.
   e. assessing, observing, and diagnosing.

   Answer: a   p. 34

7. In the clinical interview a skilled assessor can gather information from what is said and
   a. how it is said.
   b. body language.
   c. degree of eye contact.
   d. tone of voice.
   e. all of the above.

   Answer: e   p. 35

8. Unstructured clinical interviews may
   a. limit the amount of information gathered.
   b. reduce the reliability and validity of the information gathered.
   c. increase the reliability and validity of the information gathered.
   d. decrease flexibility.
   e. decrease the client's comfort level.

   Answer: b   p. 35

9. An interview schedule is typically used in
   a. an unstructured clinical interview.
   b. a structured clinical interview.
   c. psychological inventories.
   d. psychological assessment of any kind.
   e. observation.

   Answer: a   p. 36

10. Which of the following interviews contains a version for the parent and the child?
    a. The DISC
    b. The SCID
    c. The WISC
    d. The DSM-IV schedule
    e. The DISC and the SCID

    Answer: a   p. 36

11. If an assessor feels that the information gained during an interview is inconsistent with his own observations, what is the next step likely to be?
    a. Begin testing.
    b. Begin collecting observation data.
    c. Cancel further testing sessions.
    d. Collect information of a third party.
    e. Conduct the interview again.

    Answer: b   p. 36

12. If an assessor asks a client to keep a written record of when behaviors or thoughts occur, the assessor is conducting
    a. assessment.
    b. validity checks.
    c. observational research.
    d. behavioral assessment.
    e. none of the above.

    Answer: d   p. 36

13. Psychophysiological assessment consists of the measurement of one or more of
    a. the physiological processes that reflect activity in the autonomic nervous system.
    b. the physiological processes that reflect psychological functioning.
    c. the psychological processes that govern physiological behavior.
    d. the psychological processes that shape the way people think.
    e. none of the above.

    Answer: a   p. 37

14. One type of psychophysiological assessment in which the client is made attentive to small psychological changes and the psychological changes that brought them about is called
    a. EEG.
    b. MRI.
    c. biofeedback.
    d. CAT.
    e. MEG.

    Answer: c   p. 38

15. The _____ is based on x-ray technology, whereas _____ is based on magnetic technology.
    a. MRI; PET Scan
    b. CAT Scan; PET Scan
    c. CAT Scan; MRI
    d. MEG; MRI
    e. MEG; PET Scan

    Answer: c   p. 40

16. Imaging techniques like MRI, fMRI, CAT scans, and PET scans have been used to conduct
    a. basic research on emotion and cognition.
    b. applied research on mental and neurological disorders.
    c. applied research on diagnostic systems.
    d. basic research in order to map the human genome.
    e. a and b.

    Answer: e   p. 41

17. The most widely used psychological test is the
    a. MMPI.
    b. Q-sort.
    c. WISC.
    d. Rorschach.
    e. REP.

    Answer: a   p. 42

18. The MMPI is able to provide _____ based on data collected on eight clinical scales.
    a. a diagnosis
    b. a profile
    c. a thorough assessment of psychological functioning
    d. all of the above
    e. a and b

    Answer: b   p. 42

19. The MMPI works by matching a respondent's answers to
    a. answers from normal individuals.
    b. answers of people with known characteristics.
    c. the respondent's previous answers.
    d. normal or ideal answers.
    e. none of the above.

    Answer: b   p. 43

20. The most widely used self-report measure for depression is the
    a. BDI.
    b. MMPI.
    c. CBCL.
    d. TAT.
    e. TRF.

    Answer: a   p. 44

21. Which of these is *not* true about projective tests?
    a. They utilize meaningless or ambiguous stimuli.
    b. They encourage imaginative proceses.
    c. They inquire about conscious experience.
    d. They minimize reality constraints.
    e. They maximize the opportunity for unconscious concerns to surface.

    Answer: c   p. 45

22. Projective tests are most compatible with which psychological orientation?
    a. Cognitive
    b. Cognitive-behavioral
    c. Psychodynamic
    d. Rational-emotive
    e. Biological

    Answer: c   p. 45

23. The text notes one specific test that is surrounded in controversy. Which is
    it?
    a. The MMPI
    b. The Rorschach
    c. The TAT
    d. The WISC
    e. The WAIS

    Answer: b   p. 47

24. The TAT has been used in many different kinds of testing situations including
    a. assessment of achievement.
    b. diagnostic testing.
    c. behavioral assessment.
    d. structured interviewing.
    e. learning disabilities assessment.

    Answer: a   p. 48

25. Perhaps the most reliable and valid of all assessment test are the
    a. intelligence tests.
    b. personality tests.
    c. self-report inventories.
    d. projective tests.
    e. achievement tests.

    Answer: a   p. 49

26. The Wechsler intelligence tests yield three important scores:
    a. Total IQ, crystallized IQ, and fluid IQ.
    b. Total IQ, verbal IQ, and performance IQ.
    c. Total IQ, verbal IQ and behavioral IQ.
    d. Total IQ, performance IQ, and fluid IQ.
    e. None of the above.

    Answer: b   p. 49

27. The most widely used intelligence tests for children are the Stanford-Binet, the WISC, and the
    a. WAIS.
    b. TAT.
    c. Bender Gestalt Test.
    d. K-ABC.
    e. Wisconsin Card Sort.

    Answer: d   p. 50

28. If an assessor is conducting testing on an individual's memory, motor coordination, tactile and kinesthetic skills, and frontal lobe functioning, the assessor is giving
    a. functional skills assessment.
    b. intelligence testing.
    c. neuropsychological testing.
    d. personality and brain factors analysis.
    e. diagnostic testing.

    Answer: c   p. 51

29. One of the most widely used neurological testing instruments that has individuals copy figures and then draw the figures from memory is the
    a. Trail Making Test.
    b. Wisconsin Card Sorting Task.
    c. test of visual-motor integration.
    d. Wechsler Memory Scales.
    e. Bender Visual-Motor Gestalt Test.

    Answer: e   p. 51

30. A neurological test that measures an individual's ability to plan ahead, handle multiple stimuli, alternate between activities, and respond to complex visual stimuli is the
    a. Trail Making Test.
    b. Wisconsin Card Sorting Task.
    c. test of visual-motor integration.
    d. Wechsler Memory Scales.
    e. Bender Visual-Motor Gestalt Test.

    Answer: a   p. 51

31. Typical neurological testing includes giving a battery of tests. One or more examples of such batteries are
    a. the Halstead-Reitan Neuropsychological Battery.
    b. the Luria-Nebraska Neuropsychological Battery.
    c. the WCST.
    d. all of the above.
    e. a and b.

    Answer: e   p. 53

32. One criticism of both the ICD and the DSM is that they may *not* be
    a. reliable.
    b. valid.
    c. cross-culturally valid.
    d. cross-sectionally valid.
    e. cross-sectionally reliable.

    Answer: c   p. 54

33. A collection of symptoms that occur together make up
    a. a disorder.
    b. a diagnosis.
    c. a typology.
    d. a syndrome.
    e. none of the above.

    Answer: d   p. 55

34. All of these are reasons for diagnosis *except*
    a. communication in shorthand.
    b. treatment possibilities.
    c. etiologies.
    d. enabling third-party payments.
    e. all of the above.

    Answer: e   p. 55

35. Which of the reasons for diagnosis that the text describes is said to be the most important?
    a. Communication in shorthand
    b. Treatment possibilities
    c. Aid to scientific study
    d. Etiology
    e. Enabling third-party payments

    Answer: c   p. 55

36. Two psychologists test an individual and compare how similar their results and conclusions are. This is likely an example of testing
    a. inter-judge validity.
    b. inter-judge reliability.
    c. test-retest reliability.
    d. inter-judge consistency.
    e. construct validity.

    Answer: b   p. 56

37. You take an assessment test one week, and then you are asked to take it again a month later. This is likely an example of testing
    a. test-retest reliability.
    b. construct validity.
    c. predictive validity.
    d. inter-rater validity.
    e. criterion validity.

    Answer: a   p. 56

38. In terms of diagnosis, construct validity is
    a. describing and differentiating individuals with different disorders.
    b. predicting the course of a disorder.
    c. differentiating individuals with different complaints.
    d. determining whether the diagnosis captures all of the symptoms of a syndrome.
    e. none of the above.

    Answer: a   p. 56

39. The Diagnostic and Statistical Manual (DSM) was approved by
    a. the American Medical Association.
    b. the American Psychiatric Association.
    c. the World Health Organization.
    d. the International Health Organization.
    e. none of the above.

    Answer: b   p. 57

40. The DSM-IV
    a. is the most current version of the DSM.
    b. is completely reliable.
    c. has been around for 20 years.
    d. is widely accepted as the best diagnostic system ever written.
    e. is the last version of the DSM that is planned.

    Answer: a   p. 57

41. How many axes does the DSM's multiaxial system contain?
    a. Two
    b. Three
    c. Four
    d. Five
    e. Six

    Answer: d   p. 58

42. While general clinical syndromes are diagnosed on Axis I, medical disorders are diagnosed on
    a. Axis II.
    b. Axis III.
    c. Axis IV.
    d. Axis V.
    e. Axis VI.

    Answer: b   p. 58

43. Clinicians and researchers feel that the multiaxial component of the DSM is good because it allows
    a. for a broader understanding of an individual's difficulties.
    b. those diagnosing to further separate their clients into highly specific categories.
    c. for third-party payees to pay for their clients.
    d. for research to continue being collected.
    e. none of the above.

    Answer: a   p. 58

44. The co-occurrence of two or more different disorders is called
    a. codisorder.
    b. comorbidity.
    c. double disordered.
    d. multimorbidity.
    e. none of the above.

    Answer: b   p. 61

45. In the pseudopatient study described in the text, a mental hospital was informed that a person faking mental illness would seek admission, although none actually did. The study found
    a. that no new patients were identified with any confidence as faking.
    b. that more than 20 percent of new admissions were identified with confidence as faking.
    c. that more than 50 percent of new admissions were identified with confidence as faking.
    d. that at least one staff member thought each new admission was faking.
    e. none of the above.

    Answer: b   p. 62

46. All of the following are examples of culturally specific disorders *except*
    a. koro.
    b. ataque de nervios.
    c. kanji.
    d. pibloktoq.
    e. suo yang.

    Answer: c   p. 63

47. The text offers all of the following conclusions about diagnosis *except* that it
    a. is biased by a number of factors.
    b. is unnecessary.
    c. has improved.
    d. can be inaccurate.
    e. is unreliable.

    Answer: b   p. 64

48. The first type of clinical research was
    a. correlation studies.
    b. cross-sectional studies.
    c. clinical case history studies.
    d. efficacy studies.
    e. efficiency studies.

    Answer: c   p. 65

49. Outcome studies often
    a. compare different treatments to determine which is better for treating a particular disorder.
    b. track change in an individual throughout therapy to determine that therapy's effectiveness.
    c. compare rates of side effects resulting from taking two different drugs that treat the same disorder.
    d. replicate previously completed studies.
    e. none of the above.

    Answer: a   p. 65

50. In order to conduct a true experiment, you must meet two conditions:
    a. Random assignment of subjects to conditions and manipulation of at least one variable.
    b. Random assignment of subjects to conditions and measurement of at least one variable.
    c. Random distribution of gender and ethnicity.
    d. Random assignment of subjects to conditions and the ability to replicate.
    e. Random ordering of conditions and random assignment of subjects to conditions.

    Answer: a   p. 68

51. All of the following are experimental confounds *except*
    a. nonrandom assignment.
    b. experimenter bias.
    c. subject bias.
    d. observer bias.
    e. demand characteristics.

    Answer: d   p. 72

52. When can a statistically significant difference be said to have occurred?
    a. When there is less than a 95 percent probability that results were not gained by chance.
    b. When the differences are large enough to be sure.
    c. When there is at least a 95 percent probability that the results were not gained by chance.
    d. When there is no dispute about the difference among the researchers.
    e. When there is at least a 99.9 percent probability that the results were not gained by chance.

    Answer: c   p. 74

53. Problems with single-subject designs are that they are generally
    a. unreliable.
    b. invalid.
    c. ungeneralizable.
    d. not replicable.
    e. d and c.

    Answer: e   p. 75

54. An example of a comparative study is
    a. a correlational study.
    b. a cross-cultural study.
    c. a true experiment.
    d. a natural experiment.
    e. none of the above.

    Answer: a   p. 78

55. If two variables are said to be negatively correlated, as one variable
    a. increases, the other increases.
    b. increases, the other decreases.
    c. increases, the other does not change.
    d. decreases, the other decreases.
    e. decreases, the other does not change.

    Answer: b   p. 79

56. Which of the following values shows the least amount of relationship, or correlation, between two variables?
    a. .90
    b. .50
    c. .02
    d. −.30
    e. −.90

    Answer: c   p. 80

57. The most important data gathered in the ECA epidemiological study are
    a. comorbidity.
    b. lifetime prevalence.
    c. the current number of mentally disabled.
    d. the actual number of individuals currently suffering from a disorder.
    e. none of the above.

    Answer: b   p. 81

CHAPTER 3 | Psychological Approaches

1. Psychodynamic theories of personality and abnormality are so named because they stress the role of
   a. mind-body interactions.
   b. psychic movements.
   c. psychological forces.
   d. self-actualization.
   e. the unconscious.

   Answer: c   p. 87

2. According to psychodynamic approaches to abnormality, psychological well-being is associated with _____ conflicts.
   a. the absence of
   b. challenging
   c. poorly resolved
   d. unresolved
   e. well-resolved

   Answer: e   p. 88

3. Freud's version of psychodynamic theory is called
   a. analytic psychology.
   b. ego psychology.
   c. individual psychology.
   d. self psychology.
   e. psychoanalysis.

   Answer: e   p. 88

4. Psychoanalysis regards people as _____ systems.
   a. chemical
   b. energy
   c. information-processing
   d. logical
   e. physical

   Answer: b   p. 88

5. Freud stated that three forces shape human personality:
   a. Id, ego, and superego.
   b. Id, latency, and superego.
   c. Libido, latency, and ego.
   d. Libido, catharsis, and latency.
   e. Id, catharsis, and latency.

   Answer: a   p. 88

6. The id is said to be guided by
   a. the reality principle.
   b. the unconscious.
   c. the pleasure principle.
   d. hedonism.
   e. psychic energy.

   Answer: c   p. 88

7. The ego is said to be driven by
   a. the reality principle.
   b. the unconscious.
   c. the pleasure principle.
   d. Hedonism.
   e. psychic energy.

   Answer: a   p. 89

8. The presence of anxiety indicates
   a. unconscious conflict.
   b. conscious conflict.
   c. nervousness related to psychodynamic stress.
   d. all of the above.
   e. a and b.

   Answer: e   p. 89

9. Freud's term for information and impulses that are actively barred from consciousness is
   a. *displacement.*
   b. *denial.*
   c. *repression.*
   d. *short-term memory decay.*
   e. *sublimation.*

   Answer: c   p. 89

10. If you deny feeling a certain way but accuse others around you of having those feelings, you may be using
    a. repression.
    b. projection.
    c. sublimation.
    d. denial.
    e. displacement.

    Answer: b   p. 90

11. Which of the following defense mechanisms would someone use when the target of her emotions either is too threatening or cannot be reached, so she chooses a target that is less threatening and more innocent?
    a. Displacement
    b. Projection
    c. Denial
    d. Repression
    e. Sublimation

    Answer: a   p. 91

12. Denial is often used when
    a. anger is present and is making the individual feel anxious.
    b. the person that an individual is angry at is very threatening.
    c. when an individual wants to attribute stress and anxiety to someone else.
    d. when an individual does not want to face information that everyone can see.
    e. none of the above.

    Answer: d   p. 91

13. The process of channeling undesirable energies into socially desirable ones is called
    a. projection.
    b. sublimation.
    c. healing.
    d. countertransference.
    e. displacement.

    Answer: b   p. 91

14. All of the following are defense mechanisms described in the text, *except*
    a. denial.
    b. repression.
    c. sublimation.
    d. replacement.
    e. projection.

    Answer: d   p. 91

15. The idea of archetypes refers to memories from our
    a. ancestors.
    b. early lives.
    c. formal education.
    d. recent past.
    e. dream states.

    Answer: a   p. 91

16. Jung disagreed with Freud over the nature of one's _____, and Adler disagreed with Freud over the nature of one's _____.
    a. childhood; adulthood
    b. feelings; purposes
    c. social relations; instincts
    d. thoughts; behaviors
    e. unconscious mind; biological urges

    Answer: e   p. 92

17. The neo-Freudians differ from Freud in their emphasis on the _____ aspects of behavior.
    a. aggressive
    b. social
    c. irrational
    d. newer
    e. sexual

    Answer: b   p. 92

18. Contemporary versions of psychodynamic theory are somewhat diffuse and incoherent but tend to be most concerned with
    a. childhood.
    b. instincts.
    c. morality.
    d. self.
    e. unconscious processes.

    Answer: d   p. 92

19. According to modern psychodynamic theory, in what order do the major aspects of the self arise?
    a. Core self → verbal self → subjective self
    b. Verbal self → subjective self → core self
    c. Subjective self → core self → verbal self
    d. Core self → subjective self → verbal self
    e. Subjective self → verbal self → core self

    Answer: d   p. 93

20. A synonym for the core self is the _____ self.
    a. agentic
    b. authentic
    c. body
    d. emergent
    e. subjective

    Answer: c   p. 93

21. Which of the following is *not* an important feature of the core self?
    a. Agency
    b. Self-history
    c. Self-coherence in physical unity
    d. Verbal storehouse of knowledge and experience
    e. Emotions as part of oneself

    Answer: d   p. 93

22. According to self theory, which is the term used to describe people who provide support to the cohesiveness of the self throughout life?
    a. *Cathections*
    b. *Selfobjects*
    c. *Intersubjectives*
    d. *Introjections*
    e. *Therapists*

    Answer: b   p. 93

23. Which of the following is *not* seen as part of psychodynamic therapy?
    a. Transference
    b. Resistance
    c. Free association
    d. Catharsis
    e. None of the above

    Answer: e   p. 94

24. Psychodynamic therapies seek to study the _____ to correct conflicts in the _____.
    a. past; present
    b. present; past
    c. person; present
    d. past; environment
    e. none of the above

    Answer: a   p. 95

25. Psychodynamic theory is seen as
    a. an outdated system that has largely been discarded.
    b. a comprehensive description of human behavior.
    c. a long-lasting theory on the development of sexual behavior.
    d. a comprehensive theory on behavioral mechanisms.
    e. none of the above.

    Answer: a   p. 96

26. Psychodynamic theory is often criticized. Which of the following is *not* one of the criticisms described in the text?
    a. The theory is too difficult to prove or disprove.
    b. Research often fails to support psychodynamic theories.
    c. The self takes a minimal role when considering the role of sexual drives.
    d. The theory focuses too much on self, paying little attention to situation.
    e. None of the above.

    Answer: c   p. 97

27. Freud began his career as a _____. This may be why he stuck to the _____ when describing mental illness.
    a. therapist; healing arts model
    b. physician; medical model
    c. anthropologist; ethnographies model
    d. lawyer; legal interpretation
    e. psychologist; cognitive model

    Answer: b   p. 97

28. Existential theorists stress
    a. fusion.
    b. unconscious drives.
    c. thought.
    d. freedom of choice.
    e. intensive therapy.

    Answer: d   p. 98

29. Two other facets of existential theories are
    a. responsibility and thought.
    b. responsibility and capacity to will.
    c. specialness and thought.
    d. intensive therapy and use of the medical model.
    e. capacity to will and cognitions.

    Answer: b   p. 98

30. According to the existentialists, people are most afraid of
    a. aggression.
    b. choice.
    c. death.
    d. fear itself.
    e. sexuality.

    Answer: c   p. 99

31. According to the existentialists, a person who has plastic surgery to change her face to look like someone famous might be protecting herself against fear of dying through
    a. authenticity.
    b. fusion.
    c. mind-altering substances.
    d. responsibility.
    e. specialness.

    Answer: b   p. 100

32. Why is it difficult to evaluate the existential approach to personality and psychological disorders?
    a. Because it is not testable as a scientific theory.
    b. Because it is too complex to be easily understood.
    c. Because it is really just a combination of physiological positions.
    d. Because it lacks theoretical continuity.
    e. None of the above.

    Answer: c   p. 101

33. Which approach does not characterize behaviorism?
    a. Antimentalism
    b. Environmentalism
    c. Experimentalism
    d. Optimism
    e. Rationalism

    Answer: e   p. 102

34. Ivan Pavlov's first interest was in the _____ system.
    a. cardiovascular
    b. digestive
    c. immune
    d. learning
    e. nervous

    Answer: b   p. 102

35. In Pavlov's original study, what was the unconditioned stimulus?
    a. Meat powder
    b. Salivation to the meat powder
    c. Tone
    d. Salivation to the tone
    e. None of the above

    Answer: a   p. 103

36. In Pavlov's original study, what was the unconditioned response?
    a. Meat powder
    b. Salivation to the meat powder
    c. Tone
    d. Salivation to the tone
    e. None of the above.

    Answer: b   p. 103

37. In Pavlov's original study, what was the conditioned stimulus?
    a. Meat powder
    b. Salivation to the meat powder
    c. Tone
    d. Salivation to the tone
    e. None of the above

    Answer: c   p. 104

38. In Pavlov's original study, what was the conditioned response?
    a. Meat powder
    b. Salivation to the meat powder
    c. Tone
    d. Salivation to the tone
    e. None of the above

    Answer: d   p. 104

39. In classical conditioning, learning a response based on the contingency between a CS and US is called
    a. acquisition.
    b. discrimination.
    c. extinction.
    d. generalization.
    e. punishment.

    Answer: a   p. 104

40. In classical conditioning, presenting the CS alone is called
    a. acquisition.
    b. discrimination.
    c. extinction.
    d. generalization.
    e. punishment.

    Answer: c   p.104

41. Which of these is not a Pavlovian therapy?
    a. Flooding
    b. Time out
    c. Systematic desensitization
    d. Punishment
    e. b and d

    Answer: e   p. 106

42. The process by which we learn the consequences of our actions, including how we get what we want, is
    a. classical conditioning.
    b. insight learning.
    c. operant conditioning.
    d. modeling.
    e. prepared learning.

    Answer: c   p. 107

43. In his learning experiments, Thorndike employed
    a. cats.
    b. dogs.
    c. humans.
    d. pigeons.
    e. rats.

    Answer: a   p. 109

44. Positive reinforcers _____ the probability of a behavior, and negative reinforcers _____ the probability of a behavior.
    a. increase; increase
    b. increase; decrease
    c. maintain; increase
    d. decrease; decrease
    e. maintain; decrease

    Answer: a   p. 107.

45. If you shocked a subject each time he gave an incorrect response in an experiment, you would be using _____ to teach the subject not to give incorrect responses.
    a. negative reinforcement
    b. punishment
    c. positive reinforcement
    d. classical conditioning
    e. none of the above

    Answer: b   p. 107

46. The text discusses _____ as an effective treatment of self-mutilating behavior by children.
    a. extinction
    b. flooding
    c. selective punishment
    d. selective positive reinforcement
    e. systematic desensitization

    Answer: c   p. 108

47. When a therapist wants to increase the frequency of a certain behavior, a technique he could use is
    a. extinction.
    b. flooding.
    c. selective punishment.
    d. selective positive reinforcement.
    e. systematic desensitization.

    Answer: d   p. 109

48. If you ignore someone's outbursts and these outbursts decrease, your strategy can be classified as
    a. extinction.
    b. flooding.
    c. selective punishment.
    d. selective positive reinforcement.
    e. systematic desensitization.

    Answer: a   p. 109

49. The cognitive approach is _____ the behavioral approach.
    a. a descendant of
    b. a reaction to
    c. similar to
    d. a and b
    e. none of the above

    Answer: d   p. 111

50. Cognitive therapy often involves _____ one's beliefs.
    a. Acknowledging
    b. Confirming
    c. Disputing
    d. Making unconscious
    e. All of the above

    Answer: c   p. 112

51. Cognitions that explicitly anticipate future events are called
    a. attributions.
    b. appraisals.
    c. expectations.
    d. automatic thoughts.
    e. beliefs.

    Answer: c   p. 112

52. The text describes two types of expectations:
    a. Outcome and efficacy expectations.
    b. Internal and external expectations.
    c. Predictive and automatic expectations.
    d. Positive and negative expectations.
    e. None of the above.

    Answer: a   p. 112

53. An appraisal is the same thing as an
    a. attribution.
    b. automatic thought.
    c. efficacy expectation.
    d. evaluation.
    e. outcome expectation.

    Answer: d   p. 113

54. According to cognitive therapists, _____ often precede and cause emotion.
    a. automatic thoughts
    b. behaviors
    c. efficacy expectations
    d. epiphenomena
    e. outcome expectations

    Answer: a   p. 113

55. The textbook discusses all these dimensions of attributions *except*
    a. internality versus externality.
    b. stability versus instability.
    c. globality versus specificity.
    d. positivity versus negativity.
    e. none of the above.

    Answer: d   p. 113

56. Which word would rational-emotive therapists most wish to remove?
    a. *Cannot*
    b. *Cause*
    c. *Perhaps*
    d. *Should*
    e. *Would*

    Answer: d   p. 115

57. One of the most aggressive and active therapies currently in use is
    a. psychodynamic.
    b. cognitive-behavioral.
    c. rational-emotive.
    d. classical.
    e. none of the above.

    Answer: c   p. 115

58. Cognitive therapists believe
    a. that unresolved conflicts cause negative affect.
    b. that distorted thoughts cause disordered behavior.
    c. that distorted behaviors cause negative affect.
    d. that negative thoughts cause distorted behaviors.
    e. none of the above.

    Answer: c   p. 116

59. The multimodal therapy is the combination of
    a. psychodynamic and cognitive approaches.
    b. cognitive and behavioral approaches.
    c. cognitive and rational-emotive approaches.
    d. psychodynamic and behavioral approaches.
    e. rational-emotive and behavioral approaches.

    Answer: b   p. 116

60. A benefit of cognitive behavioral therapy is that it
    a. is short term.
    b. is usually inexpensive.
    c. is usually effective at treating a number of disorders.
    d. seems to be based on science.
    e. all of the above.

    Answer: e   p. 117

61. A difference between psychodynamic therapies and cognitive and
    behavioral therapies is
    a. psychodynamic therapies look at the environment as well as the
       individual, whereas cognitive and behavioral therapies do not.
    b. cognitive and behavioral therapies look at the environment as well as the
       individual, whereas psychodynamic therapies do not.
    c. psychodynamic therapies look at the here and now, whereas cognitive
       and behavioral therapies look at the past.
    d. psychodynamic therapies are short term and cost effective, whereas
       cognitive and behavioral therapies generally are not.
    e. none of the above.

    Answer: b   p. 118

CHAPTER 4

The Biological Approach and Neuroscience

1. The biological model assumes that biology is relevant to the _____ of abnormality.
   a. causes
   b. symptoms
   c. treatments
   d. understanding
   e. all of the above

   Answer: e   p. 124

2. Which model of abnormality conceives of abnormality as an illness?
   a. Biological
   b. Psychodynamic
   c. Existential
   d. Behavioral
   e. Cognitive

   Answer: a   p. 124

3. In attempting to explain the etiology of abnormal behavior, biological theorists seek to answer two questions:
   a. What caused the brain malfunction and what is the nature of the brain malfunction?
   b. What are the genetic components of the disorder and do the parents have the same disorder?
   c. What created the disorder and how best to treat the disorder?
   d. What created the brain malfunction and what is the best way to treat the disorder?
   e. None of the above.

   Answer: a   p. 126

4. Psychotropic medications have largely replaced
   a. traditional therapies.
   b. psychosurgery.
   c. ECT.
   d. a and b.
   e. none of the above.

   Answer: b   p. 126

5. A therapist who proposes that drugs can treat abnormality is working within the _____ model.
   a. biological
   b. psychodynamic
   c. existential
   d. behavioral
   e. cognitive

   Answer: a   p. 126

6. The diathesis-stress model states that _____ interact to causes mental disorders.
   a. a virus and exposure to stress
   b. a lasting condition and exposure to stress
   c. a natural predisposition and exposure to stress
   d. an unknown transference and exposure to stress
   e. none of the above

   Answer: c   p. 127

7. Neurodevelopment is generally controlled by
   a. genetics.
   b. chemicals.
   c. parents.
   d. peers.
   e. thoughts.

   Answer: a   p. 127

8. Current biomedical research suggests that there may be genetic predispositions
   a. to some mental disorders.
   b. only in abnormal brain function.
   c. to normal personality.
   d. only in twins.
   e. to some mental disorders and to normal personality.

   Answer: e   p. 127

9. Genotype refers to
   a. the outward appearance of genes.
   b. the amount of genetic information shared among siblings.
   c. the specific genes that an individual has inherited.
   d. the behavioral characteristics of genes.
   e. none of the above.

   Answer: c   p. 129

10. In terms of the amount of genetic material shared in common, which is the right order for these siblings?
   a. Identical twins = fraternal twins = nontwin siblings.
   b. Identical twins > fraternal twins = nontwin siblings.
   c. Identical twins = fraternal twins > nontwin siblings.
   d. Identical twins > fraternal twins > nontwin siblings.
   e. Identical twins > nontwin siblings > fraternal twins.

   Answer: b   p. 130

11. When one identical twin has a disorder, such as schizophrenia, and the other twin does not have the disorder, we call this _____ and attribute the cause to _____.
   a. concordant; genetics
   b. discordant; environment
   c. concordant; environment
   d. discordant; genetics
   e. none of the above

   Answer: b   p. 132

12. Currently one method used to separate the contributions to personality of learning versus genetics is to study
   a. monozygotic twins.
   b. adopted children.
   c. dizygotic twins.
   d. twins who have been separated and adopted away at birth.
   e. how monozygotic compare to dizygotic twins.

   Answer: d   p. 133

13. The twin method of study allows for a possible understanding of the roles of
   a. genetics and the type of twins.
   b. environment and the type of twins.
   c. genetics and environment.
   d. environment and phenotypes.
   e. none of the above.

   Answer: c   p. 133

14. The text describes a few other genetic study techniques, including
    a. genetic linkage analysis.
    b. cross-sectional analysis.
    c. quantitative genetic methods.
    d. a and c.
    e. none of the above.

    Answer: d   p. 134

15. Which of the following is *not* one of the parts of the neuron?
    a. Axon
    b. Synapse
    c. Soma
    d. Dendrites
    e. None of the above

    Answer: b   p. 136

16. Neuron's communicate through the use of chemicals called
    a. hormones.
    b. neurotransmitters.
    c. biofeedback loops.
    d. blood cells.
    e. cerebra-spinal fluids.

    Answer: b   p. 136

17. There are two primary types of neuronal receptors:
    a. Excitatory and inhibitory.
    b. Receptive and nonreceptive.
    c. Postsynaptic and presynaptic.
    d. Primary and secondary.
    e. Regulatory and deregulatory.

    Answer: a   p. 137

18. Which of the following is *not* one of the methods in which neurotransmitters are removed from the synapse:
    a. Diffusion
    b. Reuptake
    c. Digestion
    d. Degradation
    e. None of the above

    Answer: c   p. 137

19. The neurotransmitter most associated with Parkinson's disease is
    a. GABA.
    b. serotonin.
    c. dopamine.
    d. norepinephrine.
    e. noradrenaline.

    Answer: c   p. 138

20. Which neurotransmitter tends to increase the frequency of release during stressful situations?
    a. Dopamine
    b. Norepinephrine
    c. Adrenaline
    d. All of the above
    e. a and b

    Answer: e   p. 139

21. The body's hormones are said to affect
    a. reuptake.
    b. neuronal activity.
    c. chemical imbalances.
    d. disregulation.
    e. chemical shortages.

    Answer: b   p. 138

22. The text describes many ways in which neuronal activity can be disordered. Which of the following is *not* one of the ways?
    a. Disorder among the interconnections of neurons
    b. Disruption of the synthesis, release, and reuptake
    c. Disorder among the thoughts that lead to transmitter release
    d. Disorder of the neurotransmitters at the receptor level
    e. Disorder in the actions of hormones

    Answer: c   p. 4

23. Substances that are said to be destructive to nerves and nervous tissue are called
    a. neuropoisons.
    b. corrosive substances.
    c. plaques.
    d. tangles.
    e. neurotoxins.

    Answer: e   p. 141

24. The central nervous system contains
    a. the brain.
    b. the spinal cord.
    c. the brain stem.
    d. all of the above.
    e. none of the above.

    Answer: d   p. 143

25. The spinal cord and brain stem are most responsible for
    a. bodily sensations and the control of bodily movements.
    b. thought and reflexive motions.
    c. breathing and hormonal response.
    d. reception of audio and visual stimuli.
    e. forethought and planning.

    Answer: a   p. 144

26. The forebrain contains many of the more-developed structures, including the cortex, which is responsible for
    a. coordination.
    b. translation of stimuli to understandable input.
    c. higher-order thinking.
    d. expressed emotion.
    e. breathing.

    Answer: c   p. 145

27. Many researchers have identified areas of the brain that contribute to psychopathology. One area of the brain that contributes to anxiety, identified by Jeffery Gray, is called the
    a. behavioral inhibition system.
    b. hypothalamic-pituitary-adrenal axis.
    c. behavioral activation system.
    d. dopamine reward system.
    e. limbic system.

    Answer: a   p. 148

28. Imagine that you are in a situation in which you are confronted and very scared by a stimulus that generally makes you very anxious. Which brain area is likely to be activated?
    a. The behavioral inhibition system
    b. The hypothalamic-pituitary-adrenal axis
    c. The limbic system
    d. The fight or flight response because the fear of the confrontation will override your anxiety
    e. None of the above

    Answer: d   p. 148

29. The hypothalamic-pituitary-adrenal axis is primarily associated with
    a. anxiety.
    b. stress.
    c. depression.
    d. aggression.
    e. anger.

    Answer: b   p. 149

30. If the HPA axis is activated for a long period of time, it is likely that the person will experience
    a. increased risk for disease.
    b. increased symptoms of mental disorders.
    c. increased neuronal activity.
    d. brain degeneration.
    e. a and b.

    Answer: e   p. 150

31. The parasympathetic and sympathetic systems are located within
    a. the central nervous system.
    b. the peripheral nervous system.
    c. the somatic nervous system.
    d. the limbic system.
    e. none of the above.

    Answer: b   p. 150

32. Neurodevelopment begins in gestation and continues until
    a. adolescence.
    b. middle adulthood.
    c. childhood.
    d. old age.
    e. Midlife.

    Answer: d   p. 151

33. Researchers believe that there are critical periods of development in animals and humans. One of the most critical periods in humans is thought to be
    a. adolescence.
    b. early childhood.
    c. infancy.
    d. old age.
    e. none of the above.

    Answer: c   p. 156

34. Which of the following is believed to play a pivotal role in memory function?
    a. Explicit memory
    b. Implicit memory
    c. Crystallized memory
    d. Long-term potentiation
    e. Fluid memory

    Answer: d   p. 157

35. Explicit memory contains memories about _____, whereas implicit memory contains memories about _____.
    a. knowledge of perceptual and motor skills; specific memories of people, objects, and events
    b. intelligence; knowledge of perceptual and motor skills
    c. knowledge of specific memories about people, objects, and events; knowledge of perceptual and motor skills
    d. knowledge of perceptual and motor skills; fluid intelligence
    e. none of the above

    Answer: c   p. 157

36. Which type of memories are likely to play a role in panic disorder?
    a. Fluid memories
    b. Implicit memories
    c. Explicit memories
    d. Short-term memories
    e. Crystallized memories

    Answer: b   p. 157

37. Researchers feel that it may be difficult to separate
    a. diathesis from stress.
    b. explicit from implicit memories.
    c. nature from nurture.
    d. crystallized from fluid intelligence.
    e. none of the above.

    Answer: a   p. 157

38. It is likely that an enriched environment will benefit development because
    a. the spinal and muscle structures involved benefit from such enrichment.
    b. lack of enrichment bores an individual, thus slowing development.
    c. the sensory nervous system requires stimulation in order to develop properly.
    d. the mind cannot function in a sensory deficit environment.
    e. none of the above.

    Answer: c   p. 157

39. Stress plays a role in both psychological and _____ disorders.
    a. mental
    b. physiological
    c. psychiatric
    d. all of the above
    e. none of the above

    Answer: b   p. 158

40. Research has shown that there is no clear-cut distinction between
    a. mental health and mental illness.
    b. mental illness and physical illness.
    c. mental health and physical illness.
    d. physical health and physical illness.
    e. psychic health and physical health.

    Answer: a   p. 160

41. The distinctions that psychologists try to make, such as those between
    nature and nurture, those between genes and environment, and so on, may
    not be necessary because
    a. they do not exist.
    b. they are too simplified to apply.
    c. they are seen as occurring together, in a system, and are hard to
       distinguish from each other.
    d. they are longlasting distinctions that are well understood.
    e. none of the above.

    Answer: c   p. 160

CHAPTER 5 | Anxiety Disorders

1. Anxiety disorders are said to occur when
   a. the cognitive elements of anxiety outweigh the behavioral elements of fear.
   b. no specific object causes the disorder.
   c. the experienced fear and anxiety prevent normal functioning.
   d. the object causing fear is not recognizable.
   e. all of the above.

   Answer: c   p. 163

2. The distinction between fear and anxiety lies in
   a. the duration of symptoms caused by each.
   b. the distress about a specific object.
   c. that there are no cognitive elements in anxiety.
   d. the severity of symptoms.
   e. all of the above.

   Answer: b   p. 163

3. How were anxiety disorders classified in Freudian theory?
   a. As hysteria
   b. As an element of the Oedipal complex
   c. As a problem concerning a wandering uterus
   d. As neuroses
   e. As irrational beliefs

   Answer: d   p. 164

4. The fear response consists of all these elements *except*
   a. behavioral.
   b. cognitive.
   c. emotional.
   d. somatic.
   e. none of the above.

   Answer: e   p. 165

5. The cognitions in fear tend to concern a(n)
   a. loss.
   b. fight or flight.
   c. escape responding.
   d. threat to life and limb.
   e. applied tension.

   Answer: d   p. 165

6. The text argues that fear is a reaction to
   a. behavioral cues.
   b. danger.
   c. anxiety.
   d. somatic cues.
   e. cognitions.

   Answer: b   p. 165

7. Which of these is *not* a typical somatic reaction of fear?
   a. Accelerated respiration
   b. Flushed skin
   c. Goose bumps
   d. Increased heart rate
   e. Tensed muscles

   Answer: b   p. 165

8. A dangerous or harmful event actually occurs and a person is not there to experience it. This is an example of
   a. escape responding.
   b. fight or flight responding.
   c. avoidance responding.
   d. moderate fear responding.
   e. none of the above.

   Answer: a   p. 166

9. Avoidance responding is best described as
   a. leaving the scene after a harmful event occurs.
   b. waiting for an event to occur before fleeing the scene.
   c. leaving the scene before a harmful event occurs.
   d. not going to a scene for fear of a harmful event's occurring.
   e. leaving the scene while a harmful event is occurring.

   Answer: c   p. 166

10. Every time Henry goes to the cafeteria to eat lunch, Oscar threatens to beat him up if he doesn't give Oscar his lunch money. After a few times of this happening, when Henry approaches the cafeteria, his hands get sweaty and his heart starts to race. This is an example of
    a. avoidance responding.
    b. escape responding.
    c. classical conditioning.
    d. involuntary fear reactions.
    e. avoidance conditioning.

    Answer: d   p. 166

11. Behavior associated with fear is established through
    a. classical conditioning.
    b. instrumental conditioning.
    c. classical or instrumental conditioning.
    d. classical and instrumental conditioning.
    e. neither classical nor instrumental conditioning.

    Answer: d   p. 166

12. If a rat leaves when a signal for shock is turned on, this shows
    a. avoidance learning.
    b. escape learning.
    c. vicarious learning.
    d. all of the above.
    e. none of the above.

    Answer: a   p. 166

13. In what ways do the degrees of fear vary?
    a. By person
    b. By situation
    c. By reality of danger
    d. By both person and situation
    e. All of the above

    Answer: d   p. 166

14. John is an accountant who spends most of his time working in an office building. One night he is walking around his neighborhood and sees a mountain lion that has wandered into town from the local mountains. John experiences what psychologists would classify as
    a. high to extreme high fear based on high to extreme high reality of danger.
    b. low fear based on an extreme reality of danger.
    c. moderate fear based on low reality of danger.
    d. no fear because there is not reality of danger.
    e. extreme fear based on no reality of danger.

    Answer: a   p. 167

15. Which two types of anxiety disorders are characterized by containing experienced fear?
    a. Specific phobia and social phobia
    b. Specific phobia and post-traumatic stress disorder
    c. Phobia and post-traumatic stress disorder
    d. Phobia and obsessive compulsive disorder
    e. Post-traumatic stress disorder and generalized anxiety disorder

    Answer: c   p. 167

16. Very intense fear is phobic only if
    a. there is absolutely no actual danger.
    b. the actual danger is slight.
    c. the actual danger is moderate.
    d. the actual danger is severe.
    e. the actual danger has come to pass.

    Answer: b   p. 168

17. Phobias are all of these *except*
    a. irrational.
    b. maladaptive.
    c. socially acceptable.
    d. uncontrollable.
    e. undesirable.

    Answer: c   p. 168

18. Someone who stays inside for days at a time because she is afraid she might encounter a pigeon is probably suffering from
    a. generalized anxiety disorder.
    b. panic attacks.
    c. a specific phobia.
    d. post-traumatic stress disorder.
    e. social phobia.

    Answer: c   p. 168

19. The symptoms used to diagnose phobia include all of these *except*
    a. the fear is unreasonable.
    b. avoidance of the phobic situation or object.
    c. the fear is out of proportion to the reality of the danger.
    d. the fear pervades a number of areas of the individual's life.
    e. exposure to the phobic situation or object produces great anxiety.

    Answer: d   p. 168

20. There are five classes of specific phobias. Which of those listed below is *not* one of those classes:
    a. Animal phobias
    b. Obsessional phobias
    c. Natural, or environmental, phobias
    d. Situational phobias
    e. Blood and injury phobias

    Answer: b   p. 168

21. Phobias afflict about _____ of the population.
    a. 0.01 percent
    b. 0.13 percent
    c. 1.50 percent
    d. 11.30 percent
    e. 15.60 percent

    Answer: e   p. 168

22. A person is terrified of cats but loves dogs and fish. This person is likely
    a. a child.
    b. a male.
    c. a female.
    d. both a child and a female.
    e. both a child and a male.

    Answer: d   p. 169

23. Animal phobias usually
    a. develop in adulthood.
    b. develop in childhood.
    c. always result from a biting incident.
    d. are stable, lasting throughout a individuals life.
    e. are diffuse, applying to any animal.

    Answer: b   p. 169

24. A client goes to see a psychologist because he fears the sight of blood so much he will not go to a hospital, even when he may really need to. The psychologist determines that the client is more afraid of contamination rather than the actual sight of blood. The psychologist should
    a. diagnose the client with a specific blood phobia.
    b. diagnose the client with a contamination phobia.
    c. diagnose an obsessive-compulsive disorder.
    d. suspect an obsessive-compulsive disorder and gather more information.
    e. diagnose a post-traumatic stress disorder.

    Answer: d   p. 170

25. Inanimate object phobias share all these characteristics with animal phobias *except* that
    a. onset is sometimes related to a traumatic event.
    b. they both occur equally in women and men.
    c. they both begin in childhood.
    d. symptoms are focused on one object.
    e. b and c.

    Answer: e   p. 170

26. Which of these is *not* a common phobia?
    a. Fear of animals
    b. Fear of flowers
    c. Fear of blood
    d. Fear of travel
    e. None of the above

    Answer: b   p. 170

27. Which of these is *not* a specific phobia?
    a. Agoraphobia
    b. Animal phobia
    c. Illness/injury phobia
    d. Inanimate object phobia
    e. None of the above

    Answer: a   p. 170

28. Nosophobia is the same as
    a. agoraphobia.
    b. animal phobia.
    c. blood phobia.
    d. illness/injury phobia.
    e. inanimate object phobia.

    Answer: d   p. 170

29. Social phobia is best described as
    a. fear of touching something contaminated while outside.
    b. fear of being seen doing something embarrassing and having a panic attack.
    c. fear of shopping malls.
    d. fear of parties and group gatherings because of the social aspect.
    e. excessive worry with no real stressor.

    Answer: b   p. 170

30. People who have a social phobia are often aware that
    a. their fear is excessive or unreasonable, and so they control it.
    b. their fear is excessive or unreasonable, but they still avoid social situations.
    c. their fear is reasonable, as what they fear may actually occur.
    d. their fear is reasonable, even if others think it is not.
    e. others do not fear social situations as they do, but they feel others should.

    Answer: b   p. 171

31. Social phobia is more likely to develop in a
    a. a 9-year-old girl who is afraid to eat in public because she may vomit.
    b. a 27-year-old man who is afraid of having a panic attack while driving.
    c. a 17-year-old girl who is afraid that if people watch her she will blush.
    d. a 7-year-old boy who is afraid he will wet his pants.
    e. a 36-year-old woman who is afraid that she has gained too much weight.

    Answer: c   p. 171

32. Social phobia in Japan is likely better defined as avoiding social situations for fear of
    a. embarrassing others.
    b. humiliation.
    c. having a panic attack.
    d. blushing excessively.
    e. embarrassing the person.

    Answer: a   p. 171

33. Most people with a specific or social phobia are likely to have problems with _____ as well.
    a. depression
    b. post-traumatic stress disorder
    c. panic disorder
    d. obsessive-compulsive disorder
    e. all of the above

    Answer: e   p. 172

34. The two most common explanations for the development of a phobia are
    a. biological and Freudian.
    b. cognitive and biological.
    c. biological and behavioral.
    d. cognitive and behavioral.
    e. Freudian and behavioral.

    Answer: c   p. 172

35. What evidence exists that phobias may be genetic?
    a. Siblings are more likely than twin siblings to have phobias.
    b. Identical twins are more likely than fraternal twins to have phobias.
    c. A mother or father is more likely to have a phobia than siblings.
    d. Fraternal twins are more likely to have phobias than identical twins.
    e. Siblings raised together are more likely to have phobias than siblings raised apart.

    Answer: b   p. 172

36. Which neurotransmitters are likely to play a role in the development of phobias?
    a. Dopamine
    b. Serotonin
    c. Gamma aminobutyric acid
    d. All of the above
    e. Dopamine and serotonin only

    Answer: d   p. 172

37. Many clinicians believe that phobias develop as a result of
    a. exposure.
    b. classical conditioning.
    c. operant conditioning.
    d. modeling.
    e. shaping.

    Answer: b   p. 173

38. Little Albert came to fear the rat when it was paired with a(n)
    a. electric shock.
    b. frightening movie.
    c. loud noise.
    d. spanking.
    e. verbal rebuke.

    Answer: c   p. 173

39. What were Watson and Rayner trying to show in the Little Albert experiment?
    a. That specific phobias could be classically conditioned
    b. That specific phobias could be operantly conditioned
    c. That specific phobias were more prevalent in children that adults
    d. That specific phobias could be emotionally conditioned
    e. a and c

    Answer: a   p. 173

40. Most common phobias are highly selective to specific objects that are/were
    a. dangerous to pretechnological people.
    b. dangerous to modern people.
    c. used commonly by pretechnological people.
    d. used commonly by modern people.
    e. a and b.

    Answer: a   p. 174

41. The example in the text that states that people are more likely to react to guns as they would to houses or flowers, as opposed to snakes or spiders, demonstrates that
    a. phobias are more likely to develop to animals than inanimate objects.
    b. phobias of weapons occur as often as phobias of houses or flowers.
    c. phobias are more easily developed for things that were threats to pretechnological man.
    d. phobias are more easily developed for things occurring in nature than for human-made objects.
    e. specific phobias for weapons are hard to classically condition.

    Answer: c   p. 174

42. Fear conditioning occurs most rapidly to pictures of
    a. electrical outlets.
    b. guns.
    c. flowers.
    d. houses.
    e. snakes.

    Answer: e   p. 174

43. Prepared classical conditioning fails to explain the
    a. lack of traumatic conditioning in some phobias.
    b. irrationality of phobias.
    c. persistence of phobias.
    d. selectivity of phobic objects.
    e. susceptibility of some people but not others to phobias.

    Answer: e   p. 237

44. Prepared classical conditioning helps explain
    a. the lack of traumatic conditioning in some cases.
    b. the irrationality of phobias.
    c. the persistence of phobias.
    d. the selectivity of phobic objects.
    e. all of the above.

    Answer: e   p. 175

45. The behavioral account of phobias has trouble explaining all of these *except*
    a. the lack of traumatic conditioning in some cases.
    b. the irrationality of phobias.
    c. the persistence of phobias.
    d. the selectivity of phobic objects.
    e. none of the above.

    Answer: c   p. 175

46. How does the behavioral account of phobias explain their persistence?
    a. The phobic never tests the reality of his or her fear.
    b. The phobic constantly imagines the object he or she fears.
    c. The phobic unconsciously ruminates.
    d. The phobic periodically encounters the object he or she fears.
    e. None of the above.

    Answer: a   p. 176

47. Which is *not* a part of systematic desensitization?
    a. Counterconditioning
    b. Hierarchy of feared situations
    c. Relaxation
    d. Insight
    e. None of the above.

    Answer: d   p. 176

48. People with specific phobias can be helped by systematic desensitization
    _____ of the time.
    a. 10 to 20 percent
    b. 30 to 40 percent
    c. 50 to 60 percent
    d. 70 to 80 percent
    e. 80 to 90 percent

    Answer: e   p. 177

49. Flooding is a technique in which a person is forced to confront
    a. the US.
    b. the UR.
    c. the CS.
    d. the CR.
    e. all of the above.

    Answer: c   p. 177

50. One of the best indicators of how successful modeling will be is how
    a. much fear the model displays.
    b. much fear the client displays.
    c. successful the model expects to be at confronting the fear.
    d. successful the client expects to be at doing what the model does.
    e. long the model takes to transfer the stimulus to the client.

    Answer: d   p. 178

51. A newly developed treatment that is very effective with blood phobias
    involves
    a. exposure to gory footage.
    b. learning to draw blood.
    c. tensing muscles.
    d. cold compresses.
    e. watching others handle blood-related materials.

    Answer: c   p. 179

52. The common process underlying most effective treatments for phobia is
    a. acquisition.
    b. conditioning.
    c. discrimination.
    d. extinction.
    e. generalization.

    Answer: d   p. 179

53. People with specific phobias are likely to benefit from drug therapy
    a. only temporarily, not as a cure.
    b. as a cure, but not for temporary relief of symptoms.
    c. neither for a cure nor for relief of temporary symptoms.
    d. as an inhibitor of their experienced pain.
    e. none of the above.

    Answer: a   p. 179

54. Social phobia is best treated with which type of medication?
    a. Benzodiazepines
    b. Tranquilizers
    c. Anxiolytics
    d. Antidepressants
    e. Anti-anxiety drugs

    Answer: d   p. 179

55. Most of what we know about post-traumatic stress disorders comes from
    a. case histories.
    b. correlational studies.
    c. experiments.
    d. experiments of nature.
    e. meta-analyses.

    Answer: d   p. 180

56. Which statement regarding the precipitating trauma in PTSD is *inaccurate?*
    a. The traumatic event must be outside of the range of normal experience.
    b. There is a wide range of symptoms that are experienced with PTSD.
    c. The traumatic event is the prime causal factor in PTSD.
    d. Drugs are largely ineffective for treating PTSD.
    e. Exposure therapy is one of the better ways to treat PTSD.

    Answer: c   p. 181

57. Phobia is likely to occur through _____; PTSD is likely to occur as a result of _____.
    a. operant conditioning; confrontation with a traumatic event
    b. classical conditioning; confrontation with a traumatic event
    c. confrontation with a traumatic event; classical conditioning
    d. countertransference; confrontation with a traumatic event
    e. classical conditioning; operant conditioning

    Answer: b   p. 181

58. Which is *not* a typical aspect of post-traumatic stress disorder?
    a. Anxiety and arousal not present prior to the trauma
    b. Numbness to the world
    c. Reliving the trauma
    d. Seeking reminders of the trauma
    e. None of the above

    Answer: d   p. 182

59 A person you know was robbed at gunpoint three weeks ago and ever since he has been having nightmares recalling the event, showing anxiety about going back to the bank where he was robbed, reliving the experience in flashbacks, and reporting difficulty falling and staying asleep. What would you suspect?
a. Your friend is likely suffering from post-traumatic stress disorder.
b. Your friend should be diagnosed with post-traumatic stress disorder.
c. Your friend is likely suffering from acute stress disorder.
d. Your friend will be okay in a few days.
e. Your friend is experiencing significant anxiety but cannot be diagnosed with anything because the event was not traumatic enough.

Answer: c   p. 182

60. Your friend describes her recent experience of living through a tornado that injured two of her family members and completely decimated her family home. Given this event, which of these psychological symptoms might your friend be likely to develop?
a. Emotional numbness
b. Anger
c. Intrusive thoughts
d. Trouble sleeping
e. All of the above

Answer: e   p. 182

61. Many survivors of Nazi concentration camps report the following stress reaction symptoms *except*
a. phobic reactions to some people.
b. nightmares about the experience that continue for decades.
c. depression and crying spells.
d. aggressive feelings.
e. guilt about surviving.

Answer: d   p. 185

62. All of these events may lead to post-traumatic stress disorder *except*
a. concentration camp internment.
b. natural disasters.
c. prisoner-of-war camp internment.
d. rape.
e. none of the above.

Answer: e   p. 186

63. The text describes research showing that the Vietnam veterans most at risk for post-traumatic stress disorder were those who
    a. witnessed combat.
    b. saw their buddies killed in action.
    c. witnessed atrocities.
    d. participated in atrocities.
    e. were held in prison-of-war camps.

    Answer: d   p. 188

64. The factors that increase an individual's risk of developing PTSD following disaster include all of the following *except*
    a. neuroticism.
    b. psychoticism.
    c. a family history of mental disorders.
    d. prior combat stress reactions.
    e. a life history of mental problems.

    Answer: b   p. 189

65. If a client came to see you complaining of nightmares, jumpiness, emotional numbness, and irritability, which treatment would you feel would be most likely to succeed in the long term?
    a. Anti-anxiety drugs
    b. Antidepressant drugs
    c. Exposure treatment
    d. Stress inoculation training
    e. Supportive therapy

    Answer: c   p. 191

66. A newer treatment for PTSD is EMDR which has received
    a. validation as an effective treatment technique.
    b. scathing criticism, often compared to mesmerism.
    c. undue attention from the media.
    d. both a and b.
    e. none of the above.

    Answer: d   p. 192

67. A panic disorder is a disorder that is characterized by
    a. recurring panic attacks.
    b. a single sudden panic attack that is unexpected.
    c. a single panic attack that is expected.
    d. a and c.
    e. none of the above.

    Answer: a   p. 193

68. Panic attacks that are _____ are the defining symptom of panic disorder.
    a. unexpected
    b. situationally triggered
    c. long in duration
    d. short in duration
    e. occasional

    Answer: a   p. 193

69. Agoraphobics fear crowds because they are afraid of _____, and social phobics fear crowds because they are afraid of _____.
    a. not being able to get away; not being able to get away
    b. not being able to get away; doing something embarrassing
    c. doing something embarrassing; not being able to get away
    d. being observed; doing something embarrassing
    e. being observed; being observed

    Answer: b   p. 193

70. The most salient element of fear in panic attacks is
    a. emotional.
    b. cognitive.
    c. behavioral.
    d. physical.
    e. a and c.

    Answer: e   p. 193

71. Panic attacks typically last for several
    a. seconds.
    b. minutes.
    c. hours.
    d. days.
    e. weeks.

    Answer: b   p. 193

72. A patient comes to the emergency room complaining of chest pain, palpitations, and shortness of breath. He reports that the symptoms started suddenly while he was shopping at the mall and he has never experienced anything like them before. After a thorough physiological workup, you reassure him that he does not have a heart condition and you begin to consider a diagnosis of
    a. agoraphobia with panic attacks.
    b. generalized anxiety disorder.
    c. hypochondria.
    d. panic disorder.
    e. post-traumatic stress disorder.

    Answer: d   p. 194

73. If one twin has a panic disorder, the other twin is
    a. more likely to if they are identical.
    b. not likely to if they are identical.
    c. more likely to if they are fraternal.
    d. not likely to if they are fraternal.
    e. a and d.

    Answer: e   p. 195

74. One of the most effective long-term treatments for panic disorder is
    a. anti-anxiety drugs.
    b. SSRIs.
    c. tranquilizers.
    d. benzodiazepines.
    e. none of the above.

    Answer: b   p. 195

75. Cognitive therapists offer a differing explanation of panic disorder than the biological explanation. They believe that
    a. the fight or flight system is responsible.
    b. there is a catastrophic misinterpretation of bodily sensations.
    c. it is inherited from parents.
    d. it is caused by an overactive amygdala.
    e. it is caused by unconscious fears of the environment.

    Answer: b   p. 196

76. According to the text, the most inclusive explanation of panic disorders is the _____ account.
    a. biomedical
    b. behavioral
    c. cognitive
    d. psychodynamic
    e. none of the above

    Answer: c   p. 198

77. Both the biological and cognitive explanations of panic disorders make all of these predictions *except* that
    a. drugs are effective.
    b. inefficiency of the adrenergic system is involved in panic disorders.
    c. panic disorders are inherited.
    d. psychotherapy is effective.
    e. sodium lactate induces panic disorders.

    Answer: d   p. 198

78. According to recent research, the treatment with the greatest likelihood of success in treating recurrent panic attacks is
    a. anti-anxiety medication.
    b. antidepressant medication.
    c. sodium lactate.
    d. cognitive therapy.
    e. psychoanalysis.

    Answer: d   p. 199

79. Someone who stays inside for days at a time because she is afraid of some disaster away from home is probably suffering from
    a. agoraphobia.
    b. panic attacks.
    c. post-traumatic stress disorder.
    d. simple phobia.
    e. social phobia.

    Answer: a   p. 199

80. Agoraphobics are typically also
    a. depressed.
    b. psychotic.
    c. alcoholic.
    d. anorexic.
    e. none of the above.

    Answer: a   p. 200

81. Agoraphobics with panic attacks can be helped with
    a. antidepressants.
    b. lithium.
    c. major tranquilizers.
    d. minor tranquilizers.
    e. none of the above.

    Answer: a   p. 201

82. If your client had suffered a panic attack while driving in his car and now refuses to leave his home for fear of a recurrence, according to recent research which of the following would be your treatment of choice?
    a. Anti-anxiety medication
    b. Antidepressant medication
    c. Flooding
    d. Cognitive therapy
    e. b and c

    Answer: e   p. 201

83. Compared to panic disorder, generalized anxiety disorder (GAD) tends to be
    a. more specific in its anxiety source.
    b. somewhat more prevalent.
    c. more acute.
    d. more-readily treated.
    e. more heritable.

    Answer: b   p. 202

84. Who is more likely to be suffering from GAD?
    a. A wealthy man living in a suburban area
    b. A teenager from a middle-class family
    c. A young adult who is poor and lives in the inner city
    d. A child going to private school
    e. A mother of four, living in a suburban neighborhood

    Answer: c   p. 203

85. According to the text, in the treatment of generalized anxiety disorder, the use of anti-anxiety medication _____, while cognitive-behavioral therapy _____.
    a. produces lasting gains; produces relief only during the course of treatment
    b. produces relief only during the course of treatment; results are longer lasting
    c. lowers anxiety; elevates anxiety
    d. elevates anxiety; lowers anxiety
    e. is more experimental; is well established

    Answer: b   p. 204

86. Which of the following is *not* one of the hallmarks of the obsessions in obsessive-compulsive disorder (OCD)?
    a. Obsessions are unwelcome and distressing.
    b. Obsessions intrude on compulsions.
    c. Obsessions arise from within the person.
    d. Obsessions are very difficult to control.
    e. None of the above.

    Answer: e   p. 206

87. People with obsessive-compulsive disorder (OCD) often comorbidly suffer from
    a. bipolar disorder.
    b. depression.
    c. social phobia.
    d. schizophrenia.
    e. none of the above.

    Answer: b   p. 207

88. The text makes a distinction between obsessive-compulsive disorder (OCD) and obsessive-compulsive personality (OCP), stating that people with
    a. OCD are distressed by their symptoms; those with OCP are not.
    b. OCP are distressed by their symptoms; those with OCD are not.
    c. OCD and OCP are indistinguishable.
    d. OCD have had their disorder for a shorter period of time than those with OCP.
    e. none of the above.

    Answer: a   p. 208

89. The three predominant theories concerning OCD offer three differing views of its development. Which states that the best way to treat it is with response blocking?
    a. Biological
    b. Psychodynamic
    c. Cognitive-behavioral
    d. Rational emotive
    e. Neurological

    Answer: c   p. 210

90. There is research evidence that suggests that OCD develops after
    a. neurological insult or brain disease.
    b. brain deformity.
    c. an automobile accident.
    d. other mental illness.
    e. none of the above.

    Answer: a   p. 212

91. The most successful treatment of OCD occurs when which perspective's recommended treatments are used?
    a. Neuroscience
    b. Behavioral
    c. Cognitive
    d. Psychodynamic
    e. Rational-emotive

    Answer: b   p. 215

92. The three component views of OCD provide all of the following information *except*
    a. who will and who will not get OCD.
    b. how OCD is maintained.
    c. successful treatment methods for OCD.
    d. the physical causes of OCD.
    e. the brain structures affected by OCD.

    Answer: d   p. 215

93. Which is/are the best way(s) to treat everyday, low-level anxiety?
    a. Relaxation
    b. Mediation
    c. Over the counter drugs
    d. Prescription drugs
    e. a and b

    Answer: b   p. 217

CHAPTER 6

Somatoform and Dissociative Disorders

1. Disorders that are characterized by a loss of physical functioning as a result psychological conflict, not as a result of physical disorder, are called
   a. anxiety disorders.
   b. depressive disorders.
   c. dissociative disorders.
   d. somatoform disorders.
   e. behavioral disorders.

   Answer: d   p. 222

2. Five criteria must be met in order for a somatoform disorder to be diagnosed. Which of the following is *not* one of those criteria?
   a. A loss or alteration of physical functioning
   b. No known physical or neurological explanations for the loss or alteration
   c. Positive evidence that psychological factors are related to the symptom
   d. The patient's being often, but not always, indifferent to the loss or alteration
   e. None of the above

   Answer: e   p. 222

3. A conversion disorder is best described as occurring when
   a. physiological distress is turned into psychological dysfunction.
   b. diseases occur that are unconsciously motivated.
   c. psychological stress is turned into physical symptoms.
   d. psychological distress disappears because of a real medical condition.
   e. none of the above.

   Answer: c   p. 222

4. Briquet's syndrome is better known as
   a. conversion disorder.
   b. somatization disorder.
   c. hypochondriasis.
   d. body dysmorphic disorder.
   e. dissociative fugue.

   Answer: b   p. 223

5. A number of diagnostic criteria must be met in order for a diagnosis of somatization disorder to be given, including
   a. physical complaints must have occurred in four different areas of the body.
   b. there are complaints about a specific disease.
   c. no complaints about sexual functioning have been made.
   d. there is a distinct syndrome of psychological symptoms.
   e. all of the above.

   Answer: a   p. 223

6. Complicated medical histories without any physical basis characterize
   a. conversion disorder.
   b. somatization disorder.
   c. pain disorder (psychalgia).
   d. psychosomatic disorder.
   e. none of the above.

   Answer: b   p. 223

7. The most common somatoform disorder today is
   a. conversion disorder.
   b. somatization disorder.
   c. pain disorder (psychalgia).
   d. psychosomatic disorder.
   e. hysteria.

   Answer: c   p. 224

8. Which of the following is characterized by complaints of pain in one or more areas of the body, causing marked distress or impairment of functioning?
   a. Conversion disorder
   b. Somatization disorder
   c. Pain disorder (psychalgia)
   d. Psychosomatic disorder
   e. Hysteria

   Answer: c   p. 224

9. If an individual is experiencing high levels of anxiety and, instead of feeling the anxiety, feels a sharp, almost unbearable pain in her ankle, you, as a psychologist, would want to investigate further to decide if the individual is suffering from
   a. a somatoform disorder, likely pain disorder.
   b. an anxiety disorder, likely generalized anxiety disorder.
   c. a mood disorder, likely major depression.
   d. a real medical condition, likely a peptic ulcer.
   e. a pain disorder, but you make sure that it is none of the other disorders listed.

   Answer: e   p. 224

10. An individual goes to see a therapist with a fear of contracting a serious disease. Even though there is no good reason for believing that the individual actually has the disease, it is likely that the therapist will look toward a diagnosis of
    a. somatization disorder.
    b. hypochondriasis.
    c. pain disorder.
    d. psychosomatic disorder.
    e. conversion disorder.

    Answer: b   p. 225

11. Which of the following is *not* true about hypochondriasis?
    a. Individuals with hypochondriasis tend to dwell on bodily functions.
    b. Individuals with hypochondriasis tend to "doctor shop," seeking better medical care.
    c. The symptoms are intentionally produced, or feigned.
    d. Men and women are equally affected by hypochondriasis.
    e. Family and social life are strained for individuals diagnosed with hypochondriasis.

    Answer: c   p. 225

12. Why might it take a long time and a lot of suffering before someone gets a diagnosis of hypochondriasis?
    a. It is a fairly rare diagnosis that few know about.
    b. It takes a process of elimination, ruling out many other disorders, before the diagnosis can be given.
    c. Most psychologists do not believe that it is a real disorder.
    d. There are actual physical symptoms leading many to believe that the individual actually has the disorder he is worried about having.
    e. None of the above.

    Answer: b   p. 225

13. Which of the following is *not* true about body dysmorphic disorder?
    a. It usually begins in adolescence and, left untreated, could last a lifetime.
    b. Anorexia and bulimia are diagnoses that must be ruled out before giving the diagnosis of body dysmorphic disorder.
    c. What is considered ugly varies across culture.
    d. It is difficult to treat.
    e. None of the above.

    Answer: e   p. 226

14. Malingering is characterized primarily by
    a. the individual's having voluntary control over her symptoms.
    b. occurring in order to get some obvious goal.
    c. the individual's likely suffering from mental illness.
    d. likely occurring more often that an actual somatoform disorder.
    e. a and b.

    Answer: e   p. 227

15. Somatoform disorders are distinguished from psychosomatic disorders in terms of the _____ of the symptoms.
    a. subjective experience
    b. pattern
    c. physical reality
    d. psychological consequences
    e. severity

    Answer: c   p. 227

16. Factitious disorders are
    a. genetically determined.
    b. produced by excessive anxiety.
    c. characterized by voluntarily produced symptoms.
    d. unconsciously motivated.
    e. developed to avoid hospitalization.

    Answer: c   p. 227

17. Contemporary studies suggest that about _____ of the U.S. population has diagnosable conversion disorders.
    a. 1 percent or less
    b. 5 percent
    c. 9 percent
    d. 20 percent
    e. 25 percent

    Answer: c   p. 227

18. For which of the somatoform disorders has a clear familial link been established?
    a. Somatization disorder
    b. Conversion disorder
    c. Hypochondriasis
    d. Body dysmorphic disorder
    e. Pain disorder

    Answer: a   p. 228

19. The psychoanalytic view sees conversion disorders in terms of a conversion of _____ into _____.
    a. conscious conflicts; unconscious conflicts
    b. Eros; Thanatos
    c. id; superego
    d. psychic energy; physical symptoms
    e. wishes; reality

    Answer: d   p. 229

20. According to psychoanalytic theory, the physical loss in a conversion disorder bears a(n) _____ relationship to underlying conflict.
    a. conscious.
    b. epiphenomenal.
    c. irrational.
    d. logical.
    e. symbolic.

    Answer: e   p. 230

21. La belle indifference refers to the _____ often seen in those with a conversion disorder.
    a. lack of physical sensation
    b. lack of overt anxiety
    c. blasé premorbid personality
    d. linguistic peculiarities
    e. striking good looks

    Answer: b   p. 230

22. According to the psychoanalytic model, _____ is/are converted in a conversion disorder.
    a. biochemistry
    b. anxiety
    c. consciousness
    d. distressing actions
    e. infidels

    Answer: b   p. 230

23. The communicative theory of conversion disorders regards them as
    a. attempts to negotiate difficult interpersonal situations.
    b. contagious within families.
    c. attempts to deal with a variety of distressing emotions.
    d. results of left hemisphere damage.
    e. a and c.

    Answer: e   p. 231

24. According to the communicative theory, we expect conversion disorder to be most common among people who are
    a. alexithymic.
    b. anemic.
    c. antiseptic.
    d. arrhythmic.
    e. dyslexic.

    Answer: a   p. 231

25. According to the communicative theory of conversion disorders, symptoms change over time because they must be
    a. bizarre.
    b. interesting.
    c. plausible.
    d. psychological.
    e. sad.

    Answer: c   p. 231

26. Research suggests that hysterically blind individuals have _____ but not _____.
    a. conscious thoughts; unconscious thoughts
    b. feelings; words to express them
    c. isolated sensations; patterns
    d. percepts; awareness
    e. pupil function; nerve function

    Answer: d   p. 231

27. The percept blocking view of somatoform disorders states
    a. that perception can be block from consciousness.
    b. that somatoform disorders are a way of blocking perception.
    c. that percepts can be recognized in consciousness.
    d. that percepts cause blocking.
    e. none of the above.

    Answer: a   p. 231

28. According to the text, as a treatment of conversion disorders, _____ works only temporarily and _____ may work better.
    a. cognitive restructuring; confrontation
    b. confrontation; suggestion
    c. suggestion; confrontation
    d. hypnosis; cognitive restructuring
    e. suggestion; hypnosis

    Answer: b   p. 232

29. Psychoanalytic treatments of conversion strive for
    a. insight.
    b. positive interpersonal relations.
    c. relearning.
    d. symptom removal.
    e. symptom substitution.

    Answer: a   p. 232

30. The common thread among the more successful treatments for somatoform disorders is
    a. confrontation.
    b. suggestibility.
    c. behavior.
    d. rationalizations.
    e. none of the above.

    Answer: b   p. 232

31. *Dissociative* in dissociative disorders refers to the splitting of
    a. behavior.
    b. emotion.
    c. memory.
    d. sanity.
    e. will.

    Answer: c   p. 233

32. When one feels detachment from oneself, as if looking on oneself from outside one's body, one is likely suffering from
    a. identity confusion.
    b. amnesia.
    c. multiple personality disorder.
    d. depersonalization.
    e. derealization.

    Answer: d   p. 233

33. When an individual feels that the world is unreal and that space and time have been altered, he is likely suffering from
    a. identity confusion.
    b. amnesia.
    c. multiple personality disorder.
    d. depersonalization.
    e. derealization.

    Answer: d   p. 233

34. A fugue state in amnesia refers to
    a. intoxication.
    b. neurotransmitter abnormalities.
    c. preoccupation with music.
    d. sexual indiscretions.
    e. travel away from home.

    Answer: e   p. 234

35. Janet was brought to see her physician by her husband. He reported that ever since a catastrophic fire in their home, Janet has complained of feeling as though she is only observing herself moving through life, not actually living it. On the basis of this information, the physician tentatively diagnoses
    a. depersonalization.
    b. fugue state.
    c. derealization.
    d. identity alteration.
    e. identity confusion.

    Answer: a   p. 234

36. Retrograde amnesia is to post-traumatic amnesia as
    a. before is to after.
    b. conscious is to unconscious.
    c. etiology is to prognosis.
    d. psychological is to biological.
    e. severe is to mild.

    Answer: a   p. 234

37. Psychogenic amnesia is caused by
    a. brain injury.
    b. alcoholism.
    c. neurotransmitter abnormalities.
    d. alzheimer's disease.
    e. none of the above.

    Answer: e   p. 235

38. Dissociative amnesia often occurs to people who are experiencing
    a. family, marital, or career stress.
    b. a degeneration of brain cells.
    c. an organic brain injury.
    d. poor oxygen circulation to the brain.
    e. none of the above.

    Answer: a   p. 235

39. Which type of amnesia shows a fourfold pattern of memory loss?
    a. Psychogenic
    b. Recurring
    c. Organic
    d. Dissociative
    e. General

    Answer: d   p. 235

40. To explain psychogenic amnesia, the psychoanalytic model stresses
    _____, and the behavioral model stresses _____.
    a. anger; anger
    b. anger; anxiety
    c. anxiety; anger
    d. anxiety; anxiety
    e. anxiety; behavior

    Answer: d   p. 236

41. Recurring episodes of feeling as if a person is outside her own body,
    watching things go on around her while she is a spectator, with flat emotion
    and a lack of feeling in control, could be diagnosed as
    a. body dysmorphic disorder.
    b. somatization disorder.
    c. depersonalization disorder.
    d. dissociative fugue.
    e. derealization disorder.

    Answer: c   p. 236

42. In dissociative identity disorder, _____ almost always exists in
    some form.
    a. an eating disorder
    b. amnesia
    c. creativity
    d. depression
    e. low intelligence

    Answer: b   p. 239

43. Dissociative identity disorders always contain multiple alters or personalities, but otherwise share a lot in common with
    a. post-traumatic stress disorder.
    b. panic disorder.
    c. generalized anxiety disorder.
    d. major depressive disorder.
    e. none of the above.

    Answer: a   p. 241

44. Which statement is *true?*
    a. Men are more likely to have a multiple personality disorder than women.
    b. Women are more likely to have a multiple personality disorder than men.
    c. Men and women are equally likely to have a multiple personality disorder.
    d. Sex differences in prevalence of multiple personality disorders have fluctuated across history.
    e. Estimates of sex differences in multiple personality disorders are not available.

    Answer: b   p. 241

45. According to Bliss, the causes of a multiple personality disorder originate
    a. in one's genetic inheritance.
    b. around ages 1 to 2.
    c. around ages 4 to 6.
    d. in adolescence.
    e. in early adulthood.

    Answer: c   p. 242

46. _____ may appear in more than 95 percent of cases of multiple personality disorder.

    a. Alcoholism
    b. A history of child abuse
    c. A family history of schizophrenia
    d. Heroin abuse
    e. Inconsistent socialization

    Answer: b   p. 242

47. Psychotherapy for multiple personality disorder starts with
    a. achieving insight into causes.
    b. alleviating stress through tranquilizers.
    c. encouraging self-hypnosis.
    d. revealing different personalities to each other.
    e. teaching social skills.

    Answer: b   p. 242

48. There are still many controversies surrounding the actual existence of
    a. dissociative identity disorder.
    b. depersonalization disorder.
    c. somatization disorder.
    d. dissociative fugue.
    e. none of the above.

    Answer: a   p. 244

CHAPTER 7 | Mood Disorders

1. Many people speak of being depressed; they are not, however, clinically depressed or do not have a depressive disorder. What does this normal, everyday depression share in common with depressive disorders?
   a. The two are completely separate things; one is a clinical syndrome, whereas the other is just a normal state of mood.
   b. While sharing similar feelings or emotions, other symptoms are completely different.
   c. *Normal depression* is just a saying for a collection of feelings that surrounds a sad event or occurrence.
   d. In many ways, normal depression differs from depressive disorders in degree and severity, while sharing the same symptoms.
   e. Normal depression is cyclic, whereas depression in depressive disorders is always present.

   Answer: d   p. 250

2. The classification DSM-IV identifies a depression as chronic when it lasts without significant interruption for at least
   a. three months.
   b. six months.
   c. one year.
   d. two years.
   e. three years.

   Answer: d   p. 250

3. Double depression involves
   a. manic and depressive episodes.
   b. two depressive episodes without an intervening manic episode in a bipolar individual.
   c. a depressive episode during a dysthymic period.
   d. two depressive episodes back to back.
   e. two depressive episodes within two years.

   Answer: c   p. 250

4. Which of these statements about depression is *not* true?
   a. It is the most widespread psychological disorder.
   b. It has mild forms.
   c. Its rates have remained the same for centuries.
   d. It is associated with suicide.
   e. Individuals with depression can be helped.

   Answer: c   p. 251

5. There are four sets of symptoms that mark depression. Which of the following is *not* one of those sets of symptoms?
   a. Mood symptoms
   b. Cognitive symptoms
   c. Anatomical symptoms
   d. Motivational symptoms
   e. Physical symptoms

   Answer: c   p. 252

6. Depression may show itself in one's
   a. moods.
   b. motivation.
   c. physiology.
   d. thought.
   e. all of the above.

   Answer: e   p. 252

7. If someone is asked to describe his symptoms and states that he feels blue, sad, lonely, and hopeless, he is likely describing his _____ symptoms.
   a. physical
   b. mood
   c. cognitive
   d. motivational
   e. manic

   Answer: b   p. 252

8. Which is one of the most pervasive symptoms that affects 92 percent approximately of all depressed patients?
   a. Loss of interest or gratification in hobbies and daily activities
   b. Rapidly changing moods
   c. High, manic periods
   d. Hypomanic states
   e. All of the above

   Answer: a   p. 253

9. An example of the cognitive symptoms of depression is
   a. feeling bad.
   b. not being able to fall asleep.
   c. perceptions of loss of control.
   d. self-blame and guilt.
   e. none of the above.

   Answer: d   p. 254

10. The negative beliefs associated with cognitive symptoms of depression can cause
    a. disastrous interpersonal relations.
    b. manic attacks.
    c. loss of appetite.
    d. loss of sleep.
    e. none of the above.

    Answer: a   p. 255

11. When a depressed person describes symptoms of having trouble getting up in the morning, going to work, beginning projects, and entertaining herself, she is describing _____ symptoms.
    a. mood
    b. cognitive
    c. anatomical
    d. motivational
    e. physical

    Answer: d   p. 255

12. Over time, as depression worsens, physical symptoms begin to become apparent. Which of the following is *not* a physical symptom of depression?
    a. Weight loss or gain
    b. Sleep disturbance
    c. Loss of interest in sex
    d. Lack of arousal
    e. None of the above

    Answer: e   p. 255

13. At this moment, 1 out of every _____ Americans is severely depressed.
    a. 5
    b. 10
    c. 20
    d. 100
    e. 500

    Answer: c   p. 256

14. Epidemiological studies show that reports of lifetime rates of depression _____ with increasing age.
    a. increase
    b. decrease
    c. stay the same
    d. become more variable
    e. become less reliable

    Answer: b   p. 256

15. The text's conclusion that age is negatively correlated with lifetime risk for depression is based on
    a. case studies.
    b. cross-sectional correlational studies.
    c. longitudinal correlational studies.
    d. experiments.
    e. quasi-experiments.

    Answer: b   p. 257

16. Which of these is *not* an aspect of the relationship of age and depression?
    a. No age group is exempt from depression.
    b. The frequency of depression in the elderly is lower than in the young.
    c. The percentage of children suffering depression is decreasing.
    d. There is a trend toward younger first incidence.
    e. Those born earlier in this century report lower lifetime rates of depression.

    Answer: c   p. 257

17. Anaclitic depression refers to depression among
    a. adolescents.
    b. children.
    c. infants.
    d. the elderly.
    e. young adults.

    Answer: c   p. 257

18. The cause of anaclitic depression is
    a. harsh socialization.
    b. inconsistent socialization.
    c. permissive socialization.
    d. prolonged separation from the mother.
    e. sibling rivalry.

    Answer: d   p. 257

19. According to the text, research shows that separation from the mother
    between the ages six and eighteen months can cause an infant to experience
    a. major depression.
    b. anaclitic depression.
    c. dysthymia.
    d. mania.
    e. a depressive disorder.

    Answer: b   p. 257

20. Research has shown that rates of depression in children are _____
    rates of depression in adults.
    a. lower than
    b. higher than
    c. as high (equal to)
    d. No research has been done on this topic.
    e. The research is not yet conclusive.

    Answer: c   p. 259

21. Women with depression outnumber men with depression by _____
    to 1.
    a. 2
    b. 5
    c. 10
    d. 15
    e. 20

    Answer: a   p. 259

22. The text explains the sex difference in the rate of depression in terms of
    a. being related to biology and hormones.
    b. characteristic differences in reactions to bad events.
    c. learned helplessness in women and not in men.
    d. sex roles that describe power differentials.
    e. a number of hypotheses although the correct one is not clear.

    Answer: e   p. 260

23. Of the following descriptions, who is the *most* likely to be depressed on the basis of the data presented in the text?
    a. Jim, an African American man in his midtwenties
    b. Matt, a Caucasian boy in his late teens
    c. Linda, a Caucasian girl who is 11 years old
    d. Dana, an African American woman in her late twenties
    e. John, a Latino man in his early thirties

    Answer: c   p. 261

24. Recent stressful loss
    a. causes depression.
    b. is a risk factor for depression.
    c. makes one invulnerable to depression.
    d. and depression are unrelated.
    e. has research results that are contradictory.

    Answer: b   p. 261

25. According to research, before age _____, loss of one's mother to death may predispose adult depression, but not after this age.
    a. 3
    b. 7
    c. 11
    d. 16
    e. 21

    Answer: c   p. 262

26. In the wake of a loss, all of these protect against depression *except*
    a. a job away from home.
    b. an intimate relationship with a spouse or lover.
    c. fewer than three children to care for.
    d. religion.
    e. None of the above.

    Answer: e   p. 262

27. Moderately severe depression is expected to lift, on average, after approximately
    a. one week.
    b. one month.
    c. three months.
    d. six months.
    e. one year.

    Answer: c   p. 263

28. Very serious depressions usually lift in
    a. one week.
    b. one month.
    c. three months.
    d. six months.
    e. one year.

    Answer: d   p. 263

29. In 70 to 95 percent of all cases of a depressive episode,
    a. one can expect complete recovery.
    b. there is not a clear indication of complete recovery.
    c. the individual will suffer for longer than six months.
    d. those around the individual will also become depressed.
    e. none of the above.

    Answer: a   p. 263

30. Of people with a serious depression, about _____ do not have another in the following ten years.
    a. 1 percent
    b. 5 percent
    c. 10 percent
    d. 25 percent
    e. 40 percent

    Answer: e   p. 263

31. A pattern that may develop after the first depressive episode is
    a. a personality disorder.
    b. a chronic dysthymic disorder.
    c. mania.
    d. psychotic behavior.
    e. delusions.

    Answer: a   p. 264

32. In terms of our current state of knowledge about genetics, we can say that a depressed relative is _____ unipolar depression.
    a. a cause of
    b. a consequence of
    c. a risk factor for
    d. not an associated cause of
    e. not a risk factor for

    Answer: c   p. 264

33. Biological theories of depression focus specifically on the
    a. brain and nervous system.
    b. environmental influences on the brain.
    c. hereditary factors of mania.
    d. number of relatives with depression.
    e. onset and course of depression.

    Answer: a   p. 265

34. All of these are clues that depression involves physiological factors *except*
    a. depression is a side effect of some medications.
    b. somatic therapies are effective.
    c. depression can follow periods of physiological change.
    d. symptoms are similar across cultures.
    e. none of above.

    Answer: e   p. 266

35. Early biological theories of depression point to a(n) _____
    availability of _____.
    a. decreased; dopamine
    b. decreased; norepinephrine
    c. decreased; serotonin
    d. increased; serotonin
    e. a and b

    Answer: e   p. 266

36. Two hormone deficiencies that have been implicated in the cause of
    depression are
    a. hypothyroidism and low testosterone.
    b. high estrogen and low testosterone.
    c. hyperthyroidism and low estrogen.
    d. high testosterone and high estrogen.
    e. none of the above.

    Answer: a   p. 267

37. A system that combines neurotransmitter and hormonal abnormalities as the
    cause for depression is the
    a. caudate nucleus-adrenal axis.
    b. lateral geniculate-pituitary-thalamus axis.
    c. hypothalamus-pituitary-adrenal axis.
    d. hind brain-pituitary-adrenal axis.
    e. cortex-adrenal axis.

    Answer: c   p. 267

38. According to psychodynamic theories, depression results from
    _____ turned inward.
    a. anger
    b. anxiety
    c. doubt
    d. mania
    e. shame

    Answer: a   p. 269

39. Beck's cognitive triad refers to
    a. conscious, unconscious, and preconscious processes.
    b. negative thoughts about self, experience, and future.
    c. negative thoughts, maladaptive assumptions, and errors in logic.
    d. oughts, shoulds, and musts.
    e. id, ego, and superego.

    Answer: b   p. 269

40. According to Beck, _____ is (are) primary in depression.
    a. feelings and emotions
    b. inadequate reinforcement
    c. physiology
    d. thoughts and beliefs
    e. unconscious conflict

    Answer: d   p. 270

41. Cognitive theory suggests that depressed people make five different
    a. errors in processing of stimuli.
    b. diagnoses of what is wrong with them.
    c. errors of logic.
    d. losses of control.
    e. none of the above.

    Answer: c   p. 270

42. Helplessness is proposed as an avenue to depression by
    a. biological theorists.
    b. cognitive theorists.
    c. psychodynamic theorists.
    d. existential theorists.
    e. b and c.

    Answer: e   p. 271

43. Helplessness is produced in laboratory animals by _____ events.
    a. low frequencies of
    b. traumatic
    c. uncontrollable
    d. unpredictable
    e. unrewarding

    Answer: c   p. 271

44. Learned helplessness is shown by reduced
    a. initiation of responses.
    b. learning.
    c. suicide attempts.
    d. perseveration.
    e. a and b.

    Answer: e   p. 272

45. Learned helplessness in people is importantly influenced by
    a. attitudes.
    b. causal explanations.
    c. self-esteem.
    d. sense of humor.
    e. values.

    Answer: b   p. 272

46. Which type of explanation for a bad event lowers self-esteem?
    a. External
    b. Global
    c. Internal
    d. Specific
    e. Stable

    Answer: c   p. 272

47. Which type of explanation for a bad event leads to long-lasting helplessness deficits?
    a. External
    b. Global
    c. Internal
    d. Specific
    e. Stable

    Answer: e   p. 272

48. Which type of explanation for a bad event leads to pervasive helplessness deficits?
    a. External
    b. Global
    c. Internal
    d. Specific
    e. Stable

    Answer: b   p. 272

49. Learned helplessness and depression are parallel with respect to all of these *except*
    a. behavioral symptoms.
    b. causes.
    c. response to treatment.
    d. predisposition.
    e. none of the above.

    Answer: e   p. 273

50. Suppose you do poorly on your midterm examination. According to the learned helplessness theory of depression, which of these is the most-depressing explanation you could offer?
    a. "I was ill that day."
    b. "The test was extra hard."
    c. "I'm bad at multiple-choice tests."
    d. "I'm bad at tests."
    e. "I'm bad at school."

    Answer: e   p. 273

51. Your friend does poorly on an exam and tells you, "I just can't do math. It's hopeless; I'll never learn this stuff." According to the attributional style model, which three attribution characteristics does your friend use to explain his poor performance on the exam?
    a. Internal, stable, and global
    b. External, stable, and global
    c. Internal, stable, and specific
    d. External, stable, and specific
    e. Internal, unstable, and global

    Answer: c   p. 273

52. The MAO inhibitors work by increasing the availability of _____, tricyclics work by increasing the availability of _____, and selective serotonin reuptake inhibitors (e.g., Prozac) work by _____ the availability of serotonin.
    a. norepinephrine; norepinephrine; decreasing
    b. norepinephrine; serotonin; decreasing
    c. norepinephrine; serotonin; increasing
    d. serotonin; norepinephrine; increasing
    e. norepinephrine; norepinephrine; increasing

    Answer: e   p. 274

53. The enzyme MAO facilitates _____ of norepinephrine.
    a. the breakdown
    b. the reuptake
    c. the synthesis
    d. the absorption
    e. none of the above

    Answer: a   p. 275

54. Drugs such as those in the same class as Prozac inhibit _____ of serotonin.
    a. the breakdown
    b. the reuptake
    c. the synthesis
    d. the absorption
    e. none of the above

    Answer: b   p. 275

55. What does it mean to say that drugs like tricyclics and MAO inhibitors are "dirty drugs"?
    a. They are contaminated by other drugs.
    b. They change the availability of neurotransmitters that are not the intended targets.
    c. They are too specific in their effects.
    d. They are illegal.
    e. None of the above.

    Answer: b   p. 275

56. A newer class of antidepressants, _____, are receiving increasing attention from physicians lately.
    a. the tricyclic antidepressants
    b. the anticonvulsants
    c. the atypical depressants
    d. the prodepressants
    e. none of the above

    Answer: c   p. 276

57. Wellbutrin affects not only serotonin and norepinephrine, but also
    a. dopamine.
    b. MAO.
    c. hormones.
    d. spinal fluid.
    e. adrenaline.

    Answer: a   p. 276

58. Overall, one of the most powerful affects of antidepressants comes from
    a. the medication effects.
    b. the placebo effects.
    c. the neurochemical effects.
    d. the neurotransmitter effects.
    e. none of the above.

    Answer: b   p. 276

59. Although electroconvulsive shock as a treatment for depression presumably
    works by affecting the levels of norepinephrine in the brain, this conclusion
    is hampered because
    a. electroconvulsive shock therapy is outlawed in most states.
    b. electroconvulsive shock therapy takes too long before it is effective.
    c. mortality rates for shock therapy are too high.
    d. shock has many effects.
    e. shock therapy is mostly ineffective in alleviating depression.

    Answer: d   p. 277

60. In cognitive therapy, automatic thoughts are combated by _____
    them.
    a. stopping
    b. exaggerating
    c. ignoring
    d. ridiculing
    e. testing

    Answer: e   p. 279

61. Reattribution training in cognitive therapy aims at
    a. decreasing rumination.
    b. finding sources of blame other than the self.
    c. making explanations more accurate.
    d. all of the above.
    e. none of the above.

    Answer: b   p. 280

62. What happens to explanatory style during a successful treatment of depression?
    a. In cognitive therapy, explanatory style changes as depression lifts.
    b. In drug therapy, explanatory style changes as depression lifts.
    c. Explanatory style changes only when cognitive therapy and drug therapy are combined.
    d. Explanatory style is constant; only depression changes with therapy.
    e. a and b.

    Answer: a   p. 281

63. One dynamic therapy that has showed success in treating depression is
    a. interpersonal therapy.
    b. object relations therapy.
    c. family therapy.
    d. analysis.
    e. none of the above.

    Answer: a   p. 281

64. Research has shown that IPT is successful at preventing
    a. depression.
    b. bipolar disorder.
    c. relapse.
    d. very severe depression.
    e. dysthymia.

    Answer: c   p. 281

65. Both drug therapy and cognitive therapy for depression are effective. According to the text, drug therapy is _____, and cognitive therapy is _____.
    a. more effective; safer
    b. more likely to prevent relapse; quicker
    c. quicker; more likely to prevent relapse
    d. safer; more effective
    e. These treatments have the same effects.

    Answer: c   p. 282

66. Bipolar depression usually involves all of the following *except*
    a. manic episodes.
    b. panic attacks.
    c. mood swings.
    d. depressive episodes.
    e. impairment of functioning.

    Answer: b   p. 284

67. Which of the following is not a prominent symptom of mania?
    a. Flight of ideas
    b. Hyperactivity
    c. Distractibility
    d. Impulsive/reckless behavior
    e. Loss of appetite

    Answer: e   p. 284

68. Flight of ideas refers to
    a. distractibility.
    b. fugue state.
    c. memory loss.
    d. psychomotor retardation.
    e. suicidal ideation.

    Answer: a   p. 285

69. In terms of sleep behavior, mania manifests as
    a. deep sleep.
    b. hypersomnia.
    c. hyposomnia.
    d. insomnia.
    e. restless sleep.

    Answer: c   p. 286

70. In the United States, the lifetime prevalence of bipolar depression is
    a. 1 percent
    b. 3 percent
    c. 5 percent
    d. 7 percent
    e. 10 percent

    Answer: a   p. 286

71. Which of these statements about bipolar depression is *false?*
    a. Bipolar depression has a sudden onset.
    b. Bipolar depression recurs.
    c. Bipolar depression usually begins in early adulthood.
    d. Men are more likely to develop bipolar depression than women.
    e. The first episode is often manic.

    Answer: d   p. 286

72. Relatives of people with bipolar disorder may be
    a. angry.
    b. anxious.
    c. creative.
    d. tall.
    e. wealthy.

    Answer: c   p. 287

73. Common theories about the causes of bipolar disorder focus more on
    _____ than psychological causes.
    a. social
    b. dynamic
    c. family systems
    d. brain structures and processes
    e. none of the above

    Answer: d   p. 288

74. There is some evidence to suggest a _____ for bipolar disorder.
    a. late onset and quick recovery
    b. genetic transmission
    c. cure
    d. viral cause
    e. bacterial cause

    Answer: b   p. 288

75. The treatment of choice for bipolar disorder is
    a. electroconvulsive shock.
    b. lithium carbonate.
    c. MAO inhibitors.
    d. minor tranquilizers.
    e. tricyclic antidepressants.

    Answer: b   p. 289

76. Newer treatments for bipolar disorder include the use of _____
    because their side effects are more manageable than the side effects
    associated with lithium carbonate.
    a. antidepressants
    b. antipsychotics
    c. anticonvulsants
    d. antioxidants
    e. none of the above

    Answer: c   p. 289

77. Seasonal affective disorder is a recently described disorder based on the idea that as sunlight decreases, depression _____ and as sunlight increases, depression _____.
    a. increases; decreases
    b. decreases; increases
    c. swings to mania; decreases
    d. swings to mania; increases
    e. decreases; swings to mania

    Answer: a   p. 290

78. Seasonal affective disorder (SAD)
    a. occurs more often in men than women.
    b. is characterized by increased depression in the spring months.
    c. has been treated with mixed success using light as therapy.
    d. develops only in those with bipolar disorder.
    e. b and c.

    Answer: c   p. 290

79. If we assume that seasonal affective disorder is a valid disorder, we would expect the happiest people in the United States to live in
    a. Arizona.
    b. Michigan.
    c. Montana.
    d. New York.
    e. Oregon.

    Answer: a   p. 290

80. The segment of the population where suicide rates are growing fastest is
    a. college and high school students.
    b. elderly females.
    c. elderly males.
    d. middle-aged females.
    e. middle-aged males and females.

    Answer: a   p. 291

81. Factors that increase the risk of suicide include
    a. being male.
    b. alcoholism.
    c. advanced age.
    d. being young.
    e. all of the above

    Answer: e   p. 293

82. Perhaps _____ of suicidal individuals are significantly depressed.
    a. 5 percent
    b. 10 percent
    c. 20 percent
    d. 40 percent
    e. 80 percent

    Answer: e   p. 293

83. _____ attempt suicide more, and _____ succeed more.
    a. Men; men
    b. Men; women
    c. Women; men
    d. Women; women
    e. There are no sex differences

    Answer: c   p. 293

84. Men are more likely than women to succeed in suicide attempts because they
    a. are less likely to be depressed.
    b. are more likely to be depressed.
    c. make repeated attempts.
    d. use more lethal means.
    e. a and c.

    Answer: d   p. 293

85. Where is suicide least likely to occur?
    a. In a rural area in Africa, occupied by tribes people
    b. In a Caucasian home in the United States
    c. Amongst a group of Native Americans
    d. In an African American home in the United States
    e. None of the above

    Answer: a   p. 295

86. Suicide is most rare among
    a. children.
    b. adolescents.
    c. young adults.
    d. the elderly.
    e. none of the above.

    Answer: a   p. 295

87. The motive of _____ leads someone to suicide as a way to end distress.
    a. altruism
    b. anomie
    c. egoism
    d. manipulation
    e. surcease

    Answer: e   p. 296

88. Suicide prevention centers
    a. decrease suicide attempts.
    b. decrease successful suicides.
    c. delay suicide attempts.
    d. increase suicide attempts.
    e. have had unclear success.

    Answer: e   p. 297

CHAPTER 8 | Early-Onset Disorders

1. One challenge faced by researchers and clinicians when studying and treating childhood disorders is
   a. children can communicate their problems.
   b. children's problems are often stable and long lasting.
   c. children's problems may be developmentally dependent and they may age out of them.
   d. development occurs at similar rates for different children.
   e. all of the above.

   Answer: c   p. 302

2. Children's problems may be more difficult to understand than those of adults for all these reasons *except*
   a. children cannot always communicate their problems.
   b. children's problems are often situation specific.
   c. children's problems are usually different than normal childhood behavior.
   d. development occurs at different rates for different children.
   e. none of the above.

   Answer: c   p. 304

3. Marked deficiencies in acquisition of intellectual, communicative, and social skills characterize
   a. developmental disorders.
   b. eating and habit disorders.
   c. disruptive behavior disorders.
   d. major depressive disorders.
   e. schizophrenia.

   Answer: a   p. 305

4. Deficits in self-control that involve behavioral tendencies like hyperactivity, inattention, aggressiveness, and defiance of authority characterize
   a. developmental disorders.
   b. eating and habit disorders.
   c. disruptive behavior disorders.
   d. major depressive disorders.
   e. schizophrenia.

   Answer: c   p. 305

5. Schizophrenia among children is
   a. not possible by definition.
   b. nonexistent.
   c. rare.
   d. about as common as it is among adults.
   e. more common than it is among adults.

   Answer: c   p. 305

6. Hyperactivity is an example of _____ disorder.
   a. developmental
   b. disruptive behavior
   c. emotional
   d. gender identity
   e. habit

   Answer: c   p. 305

7. The hallmark symptom of reactive attachment disorder is
   a. delusions and thought disorder.
   b. depressive and manic episodes.
   c. an inability to relate to other people.
   d. severe anxiety about going to school.
   e. none of the above.

   Answer: c   p. 307

8. The best treatment for reactive attachment disorder is
   a. unknown as of yet.
   b. prescribed medications.
   c. cognitive behavioral therapy.
   d. psychoanalysis.
   e. a combination of therapy and medication.

   Answer: a   p. 308

9. Separation anxiety disorder is _____ reactive attachment disorder.
   a. similar to
   b. approximately the opposite of
   c. related to
   d. the same thing as
   e. none of the above

   Answer: b   p. 309

10. A child is brought to you because his parents are concerned that he seems so anxious and clingy. His parents report that he was doing fine in school until his cat was struck by a car and killed about a month ago. Since then he has suffered nightmares, often gets upset in the morning before school, and has stayed home for several weeks because of headaches and gastrointestinal symptoms. Your tentative diagnosis would most likely be
    a. separation anxiety disorder.
    b. childhood depression.
    c. avoidant disorder.
    d. school phobia.
    e. reactive attachment disorder.

    Answer: a   p. 310

11. The most common emotional disorder in children is
    a. conduct disorder.
    b. school phobia.
    c. separation anxiety.
    d. simple phobia.
    e. none of the above.

    Answer: c   p. 311

12. The first phobias to appear are of
    a. airplane travel.
    b. identity.
    c. imaginary creatures.
    d. social relationships.
    e. tangible objects.

    Answer: e   p. 311

13. The development of fears in children tends to following which of these orders?
    a. Imaginary → tangible → school connected → social relationships/identity
    b. Tangible → school connected → social relationships/identity → imaginary
    c. Social relationships/identity → school connected → tangible → imaginary
    d. Tangible → imaginary → school connected → social relationships/identity
    e. None of the above

    Answer: d   p. 309

14. Which of the following orders would represent the most likely chronology of fear development in a given child?
    a. Monsters → bees → failure → rejection
    b. Bees → failure → rejection → monsters
    c. Rejection → failure → bees → monsters
    d. Bees → monsters → failure → rejection
    e. None of the above

    Answer: d   p. 309

15. Which of the following is *not* generally associated with a school phobia?
    a. Previous good performance
    b. Hyperactivity
    c. Previous good attendance
    d. Frequent bathroom breaks
    e. None of the above

    Answer: b   p. 312

16. The treatment of choice for phobias among children stems from
    a. the biological model.
    b. the psychodynamic model.
    c. the behavioral model.
    d. all of the above.
    e. none of the above.

    Answer: c   p. 313

17. All of the following are true about childhood depression *except* that
    a. family dysfunction is a significant source.
    b. it is less common than depression in adults.
    c. a substantial minority of depressed children remain depressed for months or even years.
    d. risk factors include low self-esteem and pessimism.
    e. it is likely to develop if a child's sense of self and future are too immature.

    Answer: e   p. 314

18. A six-year-old child on the soccer team you coach seems to be sad, has low energy, and lacks confidence. You know that her parents recently separated, and she tells you that she is no longer doing well in school. Given what you remember from your college abnormal psychology class, you are particularly concerned about her because
    a. of the high rate of childhood suicide.
    b. she may now be at risk for developing autism.
    c. her depression may leave her with long-lasting negative beliefs about herself and the world.
    d. her athletic abilities may be affected.
    e. all of the above.

    Answer: c   p. 314

19. In treating emotional disorders in childhood, especially depression, it may be essential to
    a. use medication.
    b. treat it in the context of the entire family.
    c. increase secondary reinforcements.
    d. remove the child from the family.
    e. all of the above.

    Answer: b   p. 315

20. When the predominant disturbance is in the acquisition of cognitive, language, motor, or social skills, you could probably diagnose a child with
    a. attention deficit hyperactivity disorder.
    b. conduct disorder.
    c. a disorder within the pervasive developmental disorders.
    d. a disorder within the anxiety disorders.
    e. a disorder within the eating disorders.

    Answer: c   p. 315

21. An autistic boy is brought to you for assessment in a number of skill domains. In which of the following areas would you predict that he would do most poorly?
    a. Rote memory
    b. Verbal ability
    c. Spatial ability
    d. Musical ability
    e. a and c

    Answer: b   p. 316

22. What is the essential feature of autism?
    a. Hyperactivity
    b. Rote play
    c. Lack of development of an ability to respond to others prior to the age of three
    d. An inability to engage in selective play
    e. A lack of interest in rules and regulations

    Answer: c   p. 316

23. Autism has some symptoms in common with which other childhood disorder?
    a. ADHD
    b. Separation anxiety disorder
    c. Disruptive behavioral disorder
    d. Reactive attachment disorder
    e. Anorexia nervosa

    Answer: d   p. 317

24. All of the following are areas affected by autism *except*
    a. intellectual development.
    b. development of height and weight.
    c. social development.
    d. language development.
    e. insistence on sameness.

    Answer: b   p. 318

25. Most children with autism will
    a. point to objects they need rather than using language to obtain the object.
    b. use language only to get objects that they need.
    c. eventually achieve completely normal use of language.
    d. learn imaginative play.
    e. none of the above.

    Answer: a   p. 318

26. The hallmark social development symptom of autism is
    a. the constant contact with parents the patient demands.
    b. physical aloofness and distance from others.
    c. being closer to strangers than those the patient is familiar with.
    d. lack of interest in strangers who come around.
    e. becoming attached to inanimate objects.

    Answer: b p. 320

27. Which will be the likely reaction of an autistic child if her environment is changed?
    a. She will react with indifference.
    b. She will react with normal emotional distress.
    c. She will not be able to find her things.
    d. She will throw temper tantrums.
    e. She will maintain her normal rituals.

    Answer: d p. 320

28. A good prognostic predictor for autistic children is
    a. age of onset.
    b. IQ.
    c. gender.
    d. maternal age at birth.
    e. socioeconomic status of parents.

    Answer: b p. 320

29. A four-year-old child is brought to see you because his parents are concerned about his lack of responsiveness. When you ask him what his name is, he replies, "Your name is Jack." You recognize this as _____, and you begin to consider a diagnosis of _____.
    a. perseveration; autism
    b. pronominal reversal; attention deficit hyperactivity disorder
    c. pronominal reversal; autism
    d. echolalia; mental retardation
    e. echolalia; autism

    Answer: c p. 321

30. The earliest theories of autism pointed to _____ as the cause.
    a. early trauma
    b. genetics
    c. metabolic abnormalities
    d. parental aloofness
    e. social learning

    Answer: d p. 322

31. Current theorists explain autism with the _____ model.
    a. biological
    b. psychodynamic
    c. behavioral
    d. cognitive
    e. none of the above

    Answer: a   p. 322

32. Genetic research in autism has found that _____ is (are) strongly inherited, but _____ is (are) only weakly inherited.
    a. vulnerability to some cognitive impairments; the specific syndrome of autism
    b. the specific syndrome of autism; vulnerability to some cognitive impairments
    c. pronominal reversal; echolalia
    d. echolalia; pronominal reversal
    e. a and c

    Answer: a   p. 322

33. Compared to normal children, autistic children
    a. show higher rates of abnormal brain wave activity.
    b. have differences in some neurotransmitter levels.
    c. are more likely to develop epileptic seizures.
    d. are more likely to have an autistic sibling.
    e. all of the above.

    Answer: e   p. 323

34. Treatment of autism is based on the _____ model.
    a. biological
    b. psychodynamic
    c. behavioral
    d. cognitive
    e. none of the above

    Answer: c   p. 324

35. Behavioral treatments of autism are enhanced by all of these *except*
    a. those that are conducted at home.
    b. those that are intensive.
    c. those that involve parents.
    d. those that are long term.
    e. none of the above.

    Answer: a   p. 324

36. Rett's disorder occurs _____ and is believed to involve the
    _____.
    a. only in children; parents
    b. only in females; X chromosome
    c. only in males; Y chromosome
    d. only in adults; brain
    e. only in children; social environment

    Answer: b   p. 326

37. Childhood disintegrative disorder is characterized by
    a. a loss of acquired skills.
    b. a lack of development of social skills.
    c. a loss of gray matter in the brain.
    d. an inability to function in normal environments.
    e. none of the above.

    Answer: a   p. 327

38. One of the more interesting aspects of Asperger's disorder is that children
    with the disorder are usually
    a. larger than other children.
    b. smaller than other children.
    c. more mentally disabled than children with other developmental disorders.
    d. gifted in certain areas while deficient in others.
    e. younger when they are first diagnosed than children with other
       developmental disorders.

    Answer: d   p. 328

39. Mental retardation is defined in terms of
    a. low intelligence.
    b. deficits in a number of adaptive skills.
    c. manifestation before the age of 18.
    d. all of the above.
    e. a and c.

    Answer: d   p. 329

40. Why is mental retardation one of the more controversial diagnoses in the
    DSM-IV?
    a. Because no one wants his or her children to have it, so the parents fight
       the diagnosis.
    b. Because schools do not believe that mental retardation exists.
    c. Because psychologists argue over the cause.
    d. Because the DSM diagnostic criteria are very confusing.
    e. Because the disorder is based on intelligence, which is very difficult to
       define.

    Answer: e   p. 330

41. Most children who are classified as mentally retarded are _____
    mentally retarded.
    a. mildly
    b. moderately
    c. severely
    d. profoundly
    e. none of the above

    Answer: a   p. 331

42. You are asked to assess an eight-year-old child for possible intellectual
    impairment. You note that he has fallen significantly behind his classmates
    in learning, he is a little clumsy, and he seems to have difficulty understand-
    ing the social aspects of his world at school. Given this information, you
    tentatively judge him to have a _____ degree of mental retardation.
    a. mild
    b. moderate
    c. severe
    d. profound
    e. none of the above

    Answer: b   p. 331

43. Mental retardation is best thought of as a
    a. psychological disorder.
    b. phase of development that will be grown out of.
    c. disease with many possible causes.
    d. symptom with many possible causes.
    e. symptom of a specific disease.

    Answer: d   p. 332

44. Down syndrome, a form of mental retardation, stems from a problem with
    the patient's
    a. chromosomes.
    b. metabolism.
    c. neurotransmitters.
    d. respiration.
    e. vision.

    Answer: a   p. 332

45. The risk of Down syndrome increases with
    a. decreasing age of the father at conception.
    b. decreasing age of the mother at conception
    c. increasing age of the father at conception.
    d. increasing age of the mother at conception.
    e. a and d.

    Answer: d   p. 332

46. Phenylketonuria (PKU) is a problem with
    a. chromosomes.
    b. metabolism.
    c. neurotransmitters.
    d. respiration.
    e. vision.

    Answer: b   p. 334

47. Children with PKU _____ be detected by a test and _____ to prevent mental retardation.
    a. can; given medication
    b. can; operated on
    c. can; put on a special diet
    d. cannot; given medication
    e. cannot; operated on

    Answer: c   p. 334

48. Prenatal environmental factors that have been shown to influence intellectual development include all of these *except*
    a. drugs.
    b. alcohol.
    c. chronic medical conditions of the mother.
    d. maternal stress.
    e. none of the above.

    Answer: d   p. 334

49. Postnatal environmental factors that have been shown to influence intellectual development include all of these *except*
    a. ingestion of lead-based paint.
    b. accidental head trauma.
    c. physical abuse.
    d. malnourishment.
    e. none of the above.

    Answer: e   p. 334

50. Which approach to educating the mentally retarded is effective?
    a. Institutionalization
    b. Mainstreaming
    c. Segregation
    d. a and b, but particularly a
    e. b or c, depending on the severity of the mental retardation

    Answer: e   p. 335

51. Tardy development usually affects _____ skills.
    a. academic
    b. intellectual
    c. linguistic
    d. all of the above
    e. a and c

    Answer: e   p. 336

52. There is a debate whether specific developmental disorders are better regarded as psychological problems or as _____ problems.
    a. biological
    b. economic
    c. educational
    d. maturational
    e. social

    Answer: c   p. 337

53. Boys are more likely than girls to have
    a. autism.
    b. mental retardation.
    c. reading difficulty.
    d. all of the above.
    e. none of the above.

    Answer: d   p. 337

54. The primary symptoms of anorexia include all of these *except*
    a. distorted body image.
    b. loss of appetite.
    c. refusal to maintain weight at a minimally normal level.
    d. intense fear of gaining weight despite being underweight.
    e. all of the above.

    Answer: b   p. 337

55. Which of these statements about anorexia is *not* true?
    a. The prevalence of anorexia is increasing.
    b. Anorexia is more common in developed countries than developing countries.
    c. Anorexia usually begins in adolescence.
    d. Anorexics are satisfied with their extremely thin appearance.
    e. Most anorexics are female.

    Answer: d   p. 338

56. Which of the following distinguishes anorexia from bulimia?
    a. Bingeing
    b. Purging
    c. Satisfaction with appearance
    d. Onset in childhood/adolescence
    e. Menstrual problems

    Answer: a   p. 339

57. Which of the following is *not* generally a characteristic of bulimia?
    a. Bingeing
    b. Purging
    c. Feeling of a lack of control over eating
    d. Feelings of shame, distress, and helplessness
    e. None of the above

    Answer: e   p. 339

58. Bulimia is only diagnosed when an individual is
    a. overweight.
    b. average weight.
    c. underweight.
    d. fluctuating in weight.
    e. none of the above.

    Answer: e   p. 339

59. A very thin teenage girl is brought to see you because her parents are worried about her health. They believe that she goes to the bathroom after every meal and tries to throw up. She denies this and states simply that she is thin because she has been on a diet. She refuses to answer any further questions. In response to her parents' pleas for a diagnosis, you consider
    a. amenorrhea.
    b. anorexia.
    c. bulimia.
    d. enuresis.
    e. no particular disorder because there is not enough information available yet to definitively diagnose her.

    Answer: e   p. 340

60. Which of the following is *not* generally considered an explanation for the development of the eating disorders of anorexia and bulimia?
    a. Variants of mood disorders
    b. Attempts to assert autonomy
    c. The consequences of social pressures to be thin
    d. Delusional disorders
    e. The consequences of low self-esteem following abuse

    Answer: d   p. 341

61. Effective treatments for bulimia come from
    a. the biological model.
    b. the psychodynamic model.
    c. the cognitive-behavioral model.
    d. all of the above.
    e. none of the above.

    Answer: c   p. 342

62. An example of an elimination disorder is
    a. enuresis.
    b. encopresis.
    c. anorexia.
    d. bulimia.
    e. a and b.

    Answer: e   p. 343

63. Research suggests that the cause of enuresis lies in
    a. anger turned outward.
    b. classical conditioning.
    c. flawed self-control.
    d. genetic inheritance.
    e. social learning.

    Answer: d   p. 343

64. Bed-wetting is best explained by the _____ model of abnormality,
    and its treatment is best undertaken within the framework of the
    _____ model.
    a. biomedical; biomedical
    b. biomedical; behavioral
    c. behavioral; biomedical
    d. psychodynamic; biomedical
    e. psychodynamic; behavioral

    Answer: b   p. 344

65. All of these statements are true of the "bell and pad" treatment of enuresis
    except that
    a. it gives a harmless electric shock to the bed wetter.
    b. it is done at home.
    c. it is effective in 75 percent of cases.
    d. there may be some relapse.
    e. none of the above.

    Answer: a   p. 345

66. The text concludes that _____ is (are) a promising treatment(s) for stuttering.
    a. delayed auditory feedback
    b. shadowing
    c. syllable-timed speech
    d. all of the above
    e. none of the above

    Answer: d   p. 346

67. The most successful treatment for Tourette's disorder continues to be
    a. behavioral.
    b. cognitive.
    c. drugs.
    d. psychodynamic.
    e. cognitive-behavioral.

    Answer: c   p. 348

68. Violation of the rights of others most characterizes _____ disorder.
    a. attention deficit
    b. autistic
    c. conduct
    d. oppositional
    e. tic

    Answer: c   p. 349

69. Research shows that stealing is something that _____ children do.
    a. almost all
    b. most
    c. most abnormal
    d. only abnormal
    e. almost no

    Answer: a   p. 349

70. Conduct disorder is _____ across time.
    a. highly stable, equally for boys and girls,
    b. highly stable, particularly for boys,
    c. highly stable, particularly for girls,
    d. not at all stable, for boys or girls,
    e. somewhat stable, for boys or girls,

    Answer: b   p. 349

71. Conduct disorder may represent the beginning of _____ among adults.
    a. antisocial personality disorder
    b. bipolar disorder
    c. passive-aggressive personality disorder
    d. schizophrenia
    e. oppositional defiant disorder

    Answer: a   p. 350

72. Children with conduct disorders tend to come from families where discipline is
    a. harsh.
    b. inconsistent.
    c. lax.
    d. very unnoticeable.
    e. none of the above.

    Answer: d   p. 353

73. The text suggests that conduct disorders reflect _____ determinants.
    a. genetic
    b. social
    c. behavioral
    d. a and b
    e. none of the above

    Answer: d   p. 356

74. You are asked to evaluate a 14-year-old girl who has repeatedly run away from home, engaged in physical fights, and shoplifted. She is very angry and mistrustful of adults and swears at you when you ask her questions. You suspect a(n)
    a. antisocial personality disorder.
    b. attention deficit disorder.
    c. eating disorder.
    d. conduct disorder.
    e. oppositional defiant disorder.

    Answer: d   p. 357

75. In treating conduct disorder, social learning theorists have all of these goals *except*
    a. teaching adaptive new ways of problem solving.
    b. reducing the child's tendency to take the perspective of others.
    c. helping the child to learn to identify situations that may trigger aggression and hostility.
    d. lessening the child's tendency to overattribute hostility to others.
    e. none of the above.

    Answer: b   p. 358

76. Some success in treating conduct disorders results from programs based on the _____ model.
    a. biological
    b. psychodynamic
    c. cognitive-behavioral
    d. all of the above
    e. none of the above

    Answer: c   p. 359

77. Children who are hostile, negativistic, temperamental, and defiant toward authority figures may be diagnosed with
    a. antisocial personality disorder.
    b. conduct disorder.
    c. oppositional defiant disorder.
    d. ADHD.
    e. adolescent antisocial disorder.

    Answer: c   p. 361

78. Psychologists argue about whether oppositional defiant disorder and conduct disorder are
    a. disorders at all.
    b. diagnosable in children under the age of 12.
    c. too complicated to diagnose at all.
    d. different disorders.
    e. none of the above.

    Answer: d   p. 362

79. Which is *not* a typical characteristic of a child with attention deficit hyperactivity disorder?
    a. Brief attention span
    b. Energetic
    c. Restlessness
    d. School difficulties
    e. Timidity

    Answer: e   p. 362

80. A child is brought to see you because he is doing poorly in school. Although he seems bright enough when he answers your questions, he has difficulty staying still in his seat and remembering what you asked him. You begin to consider that he may have a(n)
    a. attention deficit hyperactivity disorder.
    b. attentional filter disorder.
    c. conduct disorder.
    d. learning disorder.
    e. school phobia.

    Answer: a   p. 363

81. Theories of attention deficit hyperactivity disorder focus on problems with the _____ that controls _____.
    a. central nervous system; arousal
    b. central nervous system; motor behavior
    c. hypothalamus; attention
    d. limbic system; arousal
    e. limbic system; attention

    Answer: a   p. 364

82. Hyperactive children can be calmed with
    a. antidepressants.
    b. lithium carbonate.
    c. major tranquilizers.
    d. minor tranquilizers.
    e. psychostimulants.

    Answer: e   p. 365

83. Studies show that the gains by ADHD children who have taken stimulants are _____ and the long-term prognosis for children who take these medications is _____ for those who do not.
    a. short lived; substantially better than
    b. short lived; the same as
    c. substantial; unknown
    d. long lasting; substantially better than
    e. long lasting; the same as

    Answer: b   p. 366

84. Studies show that behavioral treatments of hyperactivity are _____ in the short run.
    a. effective
    b. ineffective
    c. of unknown effectiveness
    d. frustrating
    e. cost-effective

    Answer: a   p. 367

CHAPTER 9 | Personality Disorders

1. Personality disorders refer to characteristics of a person that all of these *except*
   a. controllable.
   b. maladaptive.
   c. pervasive.
   d. stable.
   e. a source of functional impairment.

   Answer: a   p. 371

2. One characteristic of personality disorders that may be shared among those affected with personality disorders is that
   a. most people affected with personality disorders are also suffering from severe medical conditions.
   b. it has been estimated that as many as 50 percent of those who meet criteria for one personality disorder will also meet criteria for another personality disorder.
   c. the personality disorder is temporary, lasting only for brief periods of time.
   d. all those diagnosed with a personality disorder could have been diagnosed in late childhood.
   e. few of those diagnosed with a personality disorder meet criteria for any other psychological disorder.

   Answer: b   p. 372

3. The text describes three types, or clusters, of personality disorders. Which of the following is *not* one of those clusters?
   a. Odd-eccentric disorders
   b. Dramatic-erratic disorders
   c. Anxious-fearful disorders
   d. Obsessive-compulsive disorders
   e. All of the above

   Answer: d   p. 375

4. Odd ways of thinking, communicating, perceiving, and behaving may signify
   a. avoidant personality disorder.
   b. borderline personality disorder.
   c. passive-aggressive personality disorder.
   d. schizoid personality disorder.
   e. schizotypal personality disorder.

   Answer: e   p. 376

5. A 52-year-old unmarried woman tells you that she can't come to her appointment on Tuesday because the third Tuesday of every month is a bad luck day and the TV newsman told her, during last night's broadcast, that this Tuesday would be an especially unlucky one. You note that she speaks in a vague and oddly stilted way. You begin to suspect
   a. antisocial personality disorder.
   b. avoidant personality disorder.
   c. borderline personality disorder.
   d. schizoid personality disorder.
   e. schizotypal personality disorder.

   Answer: e   p. 378

6. Researchers believe that schizotypal personality disorder is related to schizophrenia on the basis of
   a. genetic studies showing that the two disorders are affected by the same genes.
   b. family studies that show that relatives of those affected with schizophrenia are more likely to have schizotypal personality disorder than those in the normal population.
   c. beliefs that schizotypal personality disorder is the same thing as schizophrenia, just misdiagnosed.
   d. lack of research support that shows that environmental influences cause schizotypal personality disorder.
   e. none of the above.

   Answer: b   p. 378

7. Someone who is unable to form social relationships and is indifferent and insensitive to others may have a(n)
   a. avoidant personality disorder.
   b. borderline personality disorder.
   c. dependent personality disorder.
   d. schizoid personality disorder.
   e. schizotypal personality disorder.

   Answer: d   p. 378

8. The treatment of choice for those diagnosed with schizoid personality disorder is
   a. cognitive-behavioral therapy.
   b. psychodynamic therapy.
   c. pharmacological treatment.
   d. strict behavioral therapy.
   e. gestalt therapy.

   Answer: a   p. 380

9. David, a 34-year-old night security guard, is brought to see you by his mother who is concerned that he does not seem to be interested in dating or getting married. During the interview, David seems reserved, distant, and unable to appreciate his mother's concerns. You begin to suspect
   a. antisocial personality disorder.
   b. avoidant personality disorder.
   c. borderline personality disorder.
   d. schizoid personality disorder.
   e. schizotypal personality disorder.

   Answer: d   p. 380

10. Which of these is (are) genetically related to schizophrenia?
    a. Borderline personality disorder
    b. Paranoid personality disorder
    c. Schizoid personality disorder
    d. Antisocial personality disorder
    e. b and c

    Answer: e   p. 380

11. Someone who is inordinately distrustful and suspicious of others may have a(n)
    a. avoidant personality disorder.
    b. borderline personality disorder.
    c. narcissistic personality disorder.
    d. obsessive-compulsive personality disorder.
    e. paranoid personality disorder.

    Answer: e   p. 381

12. A fellow at work has recently become quite hostile, accusing you of tampering with his work and secretly complaining to your mutual boss that he is incompetent because of difficulties he had with a recent project. Despite your reassurances, he has become preoccupied with this belief and has been loudly complaining to other coworkers that your "assault of hate" on him is racially motivated. You begin to suspect
    a. antisocial personality disorder.
    b. borderline personality disorder.
    c. narcissistic personality disorder.
    d. obsessive-compulsive personality disorder.
    e. paranoid personality disorder.

    Answer: e   p. 381

13. The first description of antisocial personality disorder that distinguished it from other psychological disorders in the nineteenth century termed it
    a. dementia praecox.
    b. lycanthropy.
    c. criminality.
    d. moral insanity.
    e. sociopathy.

    Answer: d   p. 383

14. Of all of the personality disorders, _____ may be the best understood.
    a. antisocial personality disorder
    b. borderline personality disorder
    c. narcissistic personality disorder
    d. obsessive-compulsive personality disorder
    e. paranoid personality disorder

    Answer: a   p. 383

15. According to Kegan's theory of antisocial personality, these individuals resemble _____ year-old children in their psychological makeup.
    a. 3-
    b. 6-
    c. 10-
    d. 13-
    e. 16-

    Answer: c   p. 383

16. Which of these is *not* part of the typical makeup of antisocial personality disorder?
    a. Antisocial behavior that makes no sense to the observer
    b. Deeply ambivalent feelings
    c. Lack of a conscience
    d. Lack of responsibility to others
    e. None of the above

    Answer: b   p. 384

17. Within Cleckley's model of antisocial behavior, a person who steals a car that he normally has permission to use would be exhibiting
    a. the absence of conscience.
    b. the absence of responsibility to others.
    c. inadequately motivated antisocial behavior.
    d. emotional poverty.
    e. sensation seeking.

    Answer: c   p. 384

18. In order for behavior to qualify as a sign of antisocial personality disorder, it must be
    a. long standing.
    b. manifested in a variety of areas.
    c. criminal.
    d. all of the above.
    e. a and b.

    Answer: e   p. 384

19. According to the text, a criminal _____ an antisocial personality disorder.
    a. may have
    b. must have
    c. as a child once had
    d. will, at some time, have
    e. none of the above

    Answer: a   p. 385

20. A new client of yours talks during therapy sessions of not feeling any guilt or shame after doing some of the things she does, such as stealing money from her mother's purse when she visits her. Within Cleckley's model of antisocial behavior, what is your client exhibiting?
    a. The absence of conscience and responsibility to others
    b. Inadequately motivated antisocial behavior
    c. Emotional poverty
    d. Sensation seeking
    e. None of the above

    Answer: a   p. 386

21. The textbook suggests that the most likely explanation for the marked sex difference in the prevalence of antisocial personality among men is
    a. that females have less testosterone.
    b. that females are more likely to commit crimes.
    c. that it reflects a true baserate difference.
    d. that males are more likely to commit crimes.
    e. a sex bias in those diagnosing individuals.

    Answer: e   p. 387

22. According to recent research, if a hypothetical case study labeled "male" was diagnosed as antisocial personality disorder, what would the identical hypothetical case study labeled "female" be diagnosed as?
    a. Antisocial personality disorder
    b. Borderline personality disorder
    c. Conduct disorder
    d. Histrionic personality disorder
    e. Narcissistic personality disorder

    Answer: d   p. 387

23. Psychological studies agree with biological studies that people with antisocial personality disorders are
    a. bad.
    b. immature.
    c. impotent.
    d. reckless.
    e. criminals.

    Answer: b   p. 387

24. Which of these early factors may *not* be a risk factor for antisocial personality disorder?
    a. Deviant behavior by father
    b. Antisocial behavior by the child, such as theft or truancy
    c. Absence of the father
    d. Parental strife
    e. None of the above

    Answer: c   p. 388

25. Adoption studies in Denmark show that the likelihood of criminality in an adopted son is significantly increased if _____ has (have) a criminal record.
    a. his adoptive father
    b. his biological father
    c. either his adoptive or biological father
    d. both his adoptive and biological fathers
    e. his biological father or both his adoptive and biological fathers

    Answer: e   p. 389

26. According to recent Danish research, which of these represents an established sex difference in the genetics of criminality?
    a. Women are more likely to be registered criminals.
    b. Men are less likely to be registered criminals.
    c. Women commit more property crimes than men.
    d. Children of convicted men are at greater risk for criminal conviction than children of convicted women.
    e. Children of convicted women are at greater risk for criminal conviction than children of convicted men.

    Answer: e   p. 389

27. The EEG studies of antisocial personality disorder suggest that these individuals have brains that are
    a. immature.
    b. large.
    c. ordinary.
    d. sluggish.
    e. small.

    Answer: a   p. 390

28. The EEG studies of antisocial personality disorder suggest problems in the _____ which controls _____.
    a. cortex; planning
    b. left hemisphere; language
    c. limbic system; emotions
    d. right hemisphere; pattern recognition
    e. a and d

    Answer: c   p. 390

29. Avoidance learning works best for psychopaths when it involves
    a. electric shock.
    b. social disapproval.
    c. monetary loss.
    d. imprisonment.
    e. starvation.

    Answer: c   p. 395

30. Someone who shows great emotion over insignificant events may have a(n)
    a. avoidant personality disorder.
    b. dependent personality disorder.
    c. histrionic personality disorder.
    d. obsessive-compulsive personality disorder.
    e. paranoid personality disorder.

    Answer: c   p. 398

31. You are asked to assess a patient who strikes you as charming and somewhat flirtatious. He almost immediately begins to describe his symptoms in a highly emotional way. You begin to consider a diagnosis of
    a. antisocial personality disorder.
    b. borderline personality disorder.
    c. dependent personality disorder.
    d. histrionic personality disorder.
    e. narcissistic personality disorder.

    Answer: d   p. 398

32. If you had to tentatively diagnose the young Scarlet O'Hara in *Gone With the Wind,* an overly dramatic girl trying to draw attention to herself, your best choice of diagnosis would be
    a. antisocial personality disorder.
    b. borderline personality disorder.
    c. dependent personality disorder.
    d. histrionic personality disorder.
    e. narcissistic personality disorder.

    Answer: d   p. 399

33. An inflated sense of self-importance and a lack of empathy are hallmarks of
    a. avoidant personality disorder.
    b. dependent personality disorder.
    c. histrionic personality disorder.
    d. narcissistic personality disorder.
    e. paranoid personality disorder.

    Answer: d   p. 399

34. An acquaintance spots you in the line at a theater and, without asking, breaks into the line and proceeds to describe how angry it made him that he was required to pay for parking to see this film when it was so inconveniently located. As you consider his behavior, you recognize its central characteristic as an overdeveloped sense of _____, and this means that this fellow may have at least some aspects of _____ personality disorder.
    a. entitlement; narcissistic
    b. evasiveness; borderline
    c. melodrama; histrionic
    d. exploitativeness; antisocial
    e. social unease; schizoid

    Answer: a   p. 399

35. Kohut suggests that narcissistic personality disorder may result when
   a. interpersonal relationships are sparse during adolescence.
   b. empathetic relationships with caregivers fail to develop.
   c. there is cognitive dissonance.
   d. unconscious conflicts within the self remain unresolved.
   e. all of the above.

   Answer: b   p. 401

36. Someone who is frequently unstable in many aspects of daily functioning including interpersonal relationships may have a(n)
   a. avoidant personality disorder.
   b. borderline personality disorder.
   c. passive-aggressive personality disorder.
   d. schizoid personality disorder.
   e. schizotypal personality disorder.

   Answer: b   p. 401

37. An individual with a borderline personality is apt to show all of these *except*
   a. chronic feelings of boredom.
   b. impulsivity in self-damaging areas.
   c. inability to express anger.
   d. mood shifts.
   e. unstable friendships.

   Answer: c   p. 402

38. *Personality* usually refers to consistencies, or stability. Which personality disorder is in this sense misclassified?
   a. Antisocial
   b. Borderline
   c. Dependent
   d. Schizoid
   e. Schizotypal

   Answer: b   p. 402

39. Theorists suggest that borderline personality disorder has its origins in _____, in experiences that _____ the self.
   a. adolescence; confuse
   b. adulthood; disappoint
   c. adulthood; humiliate
   d. childhood; fragment
   e. childhood; inhibit

   Answer: d   p. 404

40. Which therapy is seen as an effective treatment for borderline personality disorder?
    a. Cognitive-behavioral therapy
    b. Dialectical behavior therapy
    c. Psychoanalytic therapy
    d. Behavioral therapy
    e. Gestalt therapy

    Answer: b   p. 405

41. A fear of appearing foolish and a strong desire for acceptance and affection characterizes
    a. avoidant personality disorder.
    b. dependent personality disorder.
    c. histrionic personality disorder.
    d. obsessive-compulsive personality disorder.
    e. paranoid personality disorder.

    Answer: a   p. 406

42. Available evidence suggests that a diagnosis of avoidant personality disorder tells us little more than a diagnosis of
    a. generalized anxiety disorder.
    b. dependent personality disorder.
    c. social phobia.
    d. shyness.
    e. schizoid personality disorder.

    Answer: c   p. 407

43. Allowing others to make major decisions in and to take responsibility for significant areas in one's life is a possible sign of
    a. avoidant personality disorder.
    b. dependent personality disorder.
    c. histrionic personality disorder.
    d. obsessive-compulsive personality disorder.
    e. paranoid personality disorder.

    Answer: b   p. 408

44. Florence arrives at the emergency room with a broken arm and lacerations to her face. She tells you that she fell down the stairs at home but won't give any more details. When you tell her that she will have to stay in the hospital for several days for further tests, she becomes upset and says that she can't decide to stay or go home without her husband's help. She also says that he will be very upset if she is not home to cook him dinner at night. You begin to consider a diagnosis of
   a. avoidant personality disorder.
   b. borderline personality disorder.
   c. dependent personality disorder.
   d. histrionic personality disorder.
   e. paranoid personality disorder.

   Answer: c   p. 408

45. Which of the following is *not* true of people with dependent personality disorder?
   a. They may tolerate physical and/or psychological abuse.
   b. They may experience intense discomfort when alone.
   c. They may have poor self-esteem.
   d. They are more likely to be female.
   e. They often avoid companionship.

   Answer: e   p. 408

46. Which of these disorders is more common among women than men?
   a. Antisocial personality disorder
   b. Dependent personality disorder
   c. Obsessive-compulsive personality disorder
   d. Narcissistic personality disorder
   e. None of the above

   Answer: b   p. 408

47. Someone who always strives for perfection in himself and demands it from others, and is rarely pleased with the outcome of his work may have a(n)
   a. avoidant personality disorder.
   b. dependent personality disorder.
   c. histrionic personality disorder.
   d. obsessive-compulsive personality disorder.
   e. paranoid personality disorder.

   Answer: d   p. 409

48. A 40-year-old accountant is brought to see you by her husband who complains that she is cold and unexpressive, takes forever to make simple decisions, is perfectionistic, and always wants to be in control. You ask her how long they have been married and she answers, "Fourteen years, two months, and ten days." Being a keen diagnostician, you recognize signs of
    a. antisocial personality disorder.
    b. obsessive-compulsive disorder.
    c. obsessive-compulsive personality disorder.
    d. schizoid personality disorder.
    e. schizotypal personality disorder.

    Answer: c   p. 409

49. One factor that may inhibit the treatment of personality disorders is
    a. that people with personality disorders are resistant to pharmacological drugs.
    b. that people with personality disorders don't usually suffer subjective emotional distress so may not seek treatment.
    c. that clinicians often refuse to treat people with personality disorders because they are resistant to change.
    d. that those who surround a person with a personality disorder often talk him out of therapy because they do not think there is anything wrong with him.
    e. all of the above.

    Answer: b   p. 411

50. One factor that may make it difficult for clinicians to diagnose personality disorders in their clients is
    a. that the clinicians must rely on recollections of past history to meet the criteria for diagnosis.
    b. that the clinicians are not very well trained at differentiating personality disorders from abnormal behavior.
    c. that the clients often lie about their symptoms so they won't receive the diagnosis.
    d. that the diagnostic system is too strict, making diagnosis very difficult.
    e. all of the above.

    Answer: a   p. 412

51. Personality disorders are sometimes confused with _____, so it is important to understand the _____ the behaviors to ensure proper diagnosis.
    a. psychopathy; biological processes underlying
    b. anxiety disorders; motivation for
    c. normal behavior; context surrounding
    d. substance abuse; drugs affecting
    e. abnormal behavior; the psychoses.

    Answer: c   p. 412

CHAPTER 10 | The Schizophrenias

1. The myths about schizophrenia include all of the following *except* that people with schizophrenia
   a. are as normal as anyone else.
   b. are more dangerous than criminals.
   c. are necessarily disturbed throughout life.
   d. have split personalities.
   e. none of the above.

   Answer: a   p. 416

2. The myths about people with schizophrenia described in the text mainly reflect the
   a. actual symptoms of schizophrenia.
   b. contributions of genetic factors.
   c. ignorance of people who do not have schizophrenia.
   d. Judeo-Christian culture heritage of the Western World.
   e. writings of authors who have schizophrenia.

   Answer: c   p. 416

3. Schizophrenia was first described by the term _____, and it was at that time considered to be _____.
   a. *dementia praecox;* curable
   b. *dementia praecox;* incurable
   c. *psychotic reaction;* curable
   d. *psychotic reaction;* incurable
   e. *split psychosis;* curable

   Answer: b   p. 417

4. Two of the more famous researchers studying schizophrenia, Kraepelin and Bleuler, agreed that schizophrenia
   a. begins in adolescence.
   b. had no cure.
   c. was biological in nature.
   d. involved a splitting up of psychological functions.
   e. none of the above.

   Answer: c   p. 417

5. Which of these is *not* part of the DSM-IV definition of schizophrenia?
   a. Deteriorated functioning
   b. Impaired reality testing
   c. Onset after the age of 20
   d. Disturbance of psychological processes
   e. Duration of symptoms for at least six months

   Answer: c   p. 417

6. Major impairment in the understanding of reality is called
   a. dementia praecox.
   b. a hallucination.
   c. a delusion.
   d. psychosis.
   e. paranoia.

   Answer: d   p. 417

7. False beliefs that resist all argument are called
   a. dementia praecox.
   b. hallucinations.
   c. delusions.
   d. psychoses.
   e. paranoia.

   Answer: c   p. 418

8. Which of the following is *not* one of the five types of delusions?
   a. Delusions of grandeur
   b. Delusions of persecution
   c. Delusions of control
   d. Ideas of reference
   e. Delusions of paranoia

   Answer: e   p. 419

9. An individual believes that Ted Koppel is sending coded messages to him every night on *Nightline*. This is most likely
   a. thought projection.
   b. pathological narcissism.
   c. an auditory hallucination.
   d. a delusion of reference.
   e. a formal thought disorder.

   Answer: d   p. 419

10. Which kind of delusion may the belief "This exam has been designed specifically to fail you" represent?
   a. Grandeur
   b. Somatic
   c. Persecution
   d. Control
   e. Reference

   Answer: c   p. 419

11. Which kind of delusion may the belief "Your postman is manipulating your mind to deliberately make you walk funny, recite the national anthem, and think dirty thoughts" represent?
   a. Grandiose
   b. Somatic
   c. Persecution
   d. Control
   e. Reference

   Answer: d   p. 419

12. Which kind of delusion may the belief "Your brain has turned to porridge" represent (other than at exam time)?
   a. Grandeur
   b. Somatic
   c. Persecution
   d. Control
   e. Reference

   Answer: b   p. 419

13. Which kind of delusion may the belief "You are the smartest person in the world" represent?
   a. Grandeur
   b. Somatic
   c. Persecution
   d. Control
   e. Reference

   Answer: a   p. 419

14. An acquaintance of yours accuses you of trying to spike his coffee with a truth serum so that he will reveal to the CIA his closely guarded unified universe theory. You begin to wonder if he is having delusions of
    a. grandeur.
    b. somatic content.
    c. persecution.
    d. control.
    e. a and c.

    Answer: e   p. 419

15. Perceptual signs of psychosis, false sensory perceptions, are called
    a. delusions.
    b. hallucinations.
    c. dementia praecox.
    d. splitting.
    e. neurosis.

    Answer: b   p. 420

16. In schizophrenia, the most common hallucination is
    a. auditory.
    b. gustatory.
    c. olfactory.
    d. tactile.
    e. visual.

    Answer: a   p. 420

17. The major difference between dreams and hallucinations is
    a. their content.
    b. when one has them.
    c. where one has them.
    d. who has them.
    e. all of the above.

    Answer: b   p. 420

18. People with schizophrenia who are experiencing hallucinations often
    a. talk to themselves or deities.
    b. sleep through them thinking they are dreams.
    c. ignore them because they do not seem real.
    d. tell others about them.
    e. none of the above.

    Answer: a   p. 420

19. Research suggests that people who have schizophrenia with hallucinations are those who have
    a. lesions in the visual cortex.
    b. low intelligence.
    c. active imaginations.
    d. the worst prognosis.
    e. trouble distinguishing internal and external events.

    Answer: e   p. 420

20. Speech that switches from topic to topic with no apparent connection is called
    a. derailment.
    b. neologism.
    c. word salad.
    d. flight of ideas.
    e. clang associations.

    Answer: a   p. 422

21. "The lazy, crazy, hazy days of summer" exemplifies a(n)
    a. clang association.
    b. flight of ideas.
    c. idea of reference.
    d. neologism.
    e. word salad.

    Answer: a   p. 422

22. If you asked a patient, "Why did you come to the hospital?" and she answered, "I had seesums," this would be an example of
    a. clang association.
    b. flight of ideas.
    c. idea of reference.
    d. neologism.
    e. word salad.

    Answer: d   p. 422

23. The disorganized speech in schizophrenia is thought to be caused by
    a. the environment.
    b. low intelligence.
    c. the disorder itself.
    d. lack of education.
    e. birth defects.

    Answer: c   p. 423

24. Which of the following is *not* commonly called disorganized or catatonic behavior?
    a. Bizarre giddiness
    b. Excitement
    c. Extreme irritability and agitation
    d. Decreased movement
    e. All of the above

    Answer: e   p. 423

25. _____ are characterized by a reduction in normal behavior, while _____ are characterized by an excess of sensory perceptions and ideas.
    a. Negative symptoms; positive symptoms
    b. Positive symptoms; negative symptoms
    c. Catatonic symptoms; hallucinations
    d. Negative symptoms; disorganized symptoms
    e. Catatonic symptoms; positive symptoms

    Answer: a   p. 423

26. Which of the following would *not* be a positive symptom in schizophrenia?
    a. Hallucinations
    b. Delusions
    c. Muteness
    d. Clang associations
    e. None of the above

    Answer: c   p. 423

27. Which of the following would *not* be a negative symptom in schizophrenia?
    a. Thought disorder
    b. Apathy
    c. Flat affect
    d. Avolition
    e. None of the above

    Answer: a   p. 423

28. One of the most common negative symptoms of schizophrenia is
    a. marked decrease in movement.
    b. disorganized behavior.
    c. flattened, or blunted, affect.
    d. clang associations.
    e. tangential thoughts.

    Answer: c   p. 423

29. Marked decrease in speech is called
    a. a catatonic symptom.
    b. tangential thoughts.
    c. alogia.
    d. avolition.
    e. disorganized behavior.

    Answer: c   p. 423

30. Unawareness of symptoms, called _____, is a hallmark of schizophrenia
    a. alogia
    b. anosognosia
    c. avolition
    d. blunted affect
    e. tangential thoughts

    Answer: b   p. 424

31. Which is the most common cause of death among people diagnosed with schizophrenia?
    a. The disease itself
    b. Catatonia
    c. Overmedication
    d. Suicide
    e. Persecution

    Answer: d   p. 424

32. The most common disorder comorbidly occurring with schizophrenia is
    a. substance abuse.
    b. depression.
    c. bipolar disorder.
    d. obsessive-compulsive disorder.
    e. none of the above.

    Answer: b   p. 424

33. Which of the following is *not* one of the subtypes of schizophrenia?
    a. Paranoid
    b. Residual
    c. Prodromal
    d. Catatonic
    e. Disorganized

    Answer: c   p. 425

34. Suspiciousness characterizes _____ schizophrenia.
    a. catatonic
    b. disorganized
    c. paranoid
    d. residual
    e. undifferentiated

    Answer: c   p. 425

35. If a patient diagnosed with schizophrenia eyed you guardedly when you entered her room and got extremely agitated when you looked at her chart, you might begin to consider a subtype diagnosis of
    a. catatonic.
    b. disorganized.
    c. paranoid.
    d. residual.
    e. undifferentiated.

    Answer: c   p. 426

36. Silliness and incoherence, bursting into laughter, grimacing, and giggling without appropriate stimuli characterize _____ schizophrenia.
    a. catatonic
    b. disorganized
    c. paranoid
    d. residual
    e. undifferentiated

    Answer: b   p. 426

37. If a patient with schizophrenia laughed uncontrollably and spoke gibberish when you entered his room, you might consider a subtype diagnosis of
    a. catatonic.
    b. disorganized.
    c. paranoid.
    d. residual.
    e. undifferentiated.

    Answer: b   p. 426

38. Bizarre motor behavior, either enormously excited or strikingly frozen, characterizes _____ schizophrenia.
    a. catatonic
    b. disorganized
    c. paranoid
    d. residual
    e. undifferentiated

    Answer: a   p. 426

39. If a patient with schizophrenia seemed agitated one day and stood uncomfortably frozen on another, you might consider a subtype diagnosis of
    a. catatonic.
    b. disorganized.
    c. paranoid.
    d. residual.
    e. undifferentiated.

    Answer: a   p. 426

40. Negativism, the apparently motiveless resistance to all instructions, characterizes _____ schizophrenia.
    a. catatonic
    b. disorganized
    c. paranoid
    d. residual
    e. undifferentiated

    Answer: a   p. 427

41. Absence of the prominent symptoms of the other subtypes of schizophrenia characterizes _____ schizophrenia.
    a. catatonic
    b. disorganized
    c. paranoid
    d. residual
    e. undifferentiated

    Answer: e   p. 427

42. If a previously schizophrenic patient reported no delusions or hallucinations but you noted that she seemed apathetic, emotionally flat, and her grooming was noticeably poor, you might consider a subtype diagnosis of
    a. catatonic.
    b. disorganized.
    c. paranoid.
    d. residual.
    e. undifferentiated.

    Answer: d   p. 427

43. Which of the following is a common symptom of undifferentiated schizophrenia?
    a. Paranoia
    b. Catatonia
    c. Depression
    d. Apathy or lack of initiative
    e. Suicidality

    Answer: d   p. 427

44. Acute schizophrenia is to chronic schizophrenia as
    a. many episodes is to few episodes.
    b. less serious is to more serious.
    c. sudden is to gradual.
    d. symptomatic is to asymptomatic.
    e. female is to male.

    Answer: c   p. 427

45. How do the prognoses of Type I and Type II schizophrenia compare?
    a. Type I has a worse prognosis than Type II.
    b. Type I has a better prognosis than Type II.
    c. Type I and Type II have the same prognosis.
    d. Research results are contradictory.
    e. Prognosis depends on other factors.

    Answer: b   p. 428

46. Type I schizophrenia is characterized by _____ whereas Type II
    schizophrenia is characterized by _____.
    a. acute schizophrenia; chronic schizophrenia
    b. biological; psychological
    c. mild; severe
    d. positive symptoms; negative symptoms
    e. catatonic; paranoid

    Answer: d   p. 428

47. One cognitive function that seems to be especially impaired in people
    diagnosed with schizophrenia is
    a. memory.
    b. language.
    c. sensory processing.
    d. intelligence.
    e. overinclusiveness.

    Answer: a   p. 431

48. Theorists speculate that schizophrenia involves a(n) _____ in the
    attentional cognitive filter.
    a. breakdown
    b. hyperefficiency
    c. inconsistency
    d. inefficiency
    e. narrowness

    Answer: a   p. 432

49. A clear example of perceptual deficits, characterized by sensory processing impairment, is
    a. a breakdown of the cognitive filter.
    b. longer time periods on backward masking tasks.
    c. below normal IQ scores.
    d. auditory hallucinations.
    e. a lack of cognitive comprehension.

    Answer: b   p. 434

50. People diagnosed with schizophrenia tend to score lower on
    a. tests of motor functioning.
    b. intelligence tests.
    c. tests of reality.
    d. depression inventories.
    e. all of the above.

    Answer: a   p. 435

51. Research evidence suggests that people diagnosed with schizophrenia have difficulty processing and understanding
    a. simple sensory information related to color and texture.
    b. facial expressions.
    c. medical information.
    d. laboratory results.
    e. all of the above.

    Answer: b   p. 435

52. In Gottesman and Shields's study concerning the concordance of schizophrenia in twins, they found that
    a. concordance in identical twins is 100 percent.
    b. concordance in identical twins is the same as in fraternal twins.
    c. fraternal twins are more concordant than identical twins.
    d. identical twins are more concordant than fraternal twins.
    e. both a and d.

    Answer: d   p. 437

53. In studies of the genetics of schizophrenia and other disorders, the first member of a family to be identified with the disorder is called the
    a. at-risk individual.
    b. co-twin.
    c. identified patient.
    d. reference case.
    e. proband.

    Answer: e   p. 437

54. Schizophrenia occurs at the rate of _____ among monozygotic twins.
    a. 1 percent
    b. 5 percent
    c. 10 percent
    d. 25 percent
    e. 50 percent

    Answer: e   p. 438

55. The concordance of schizophrenia among ordinary siblings is about
    a. 1 percent.
    b. 5 percent.
    c. 10 percent.
    d. 25 percent.
    e. 50 percent.

    Answer: c   p. 439

56. If an individual has _____ who has schizophrenia, his or her chances of having schizophrenia are greatest.
    a. a brother
    b. a fraternal twin
    c. a sister
    d. an identical twin
    e. two parents

    Answer: d   p. 439

57. When researchers report that the risk of schizophrenia to the relatives of a schizophrenic increases markedly with the degree of genetic relatedness, we can expect that
    a. a fraternal twin (DZ) of a schizophrenic proband will be more likely to develop the illness than a sibling of the proband will.
    b. a grandchild of a schizophrenic will be more likely to develop the illness than a child of a schizophrenic will.
    c. an identical twin (MZ) of a schizophrenic proband will be more likely to develop the illness than a fraternal twin (DZ) of the proband will.
    d. a fraternal twin (DZ) of a schizophrenic proband will be more likely to develop the illness than an identical twin (MZ) of the proband will.
    e. schizophrenia is more likely to develop in a child of a schizophrenic than in a parent of a schizophrenic.

    Answer: c   p. 439

58. If you wanted to rule out the contribution of environmental factors to the etiology of schizophrenia, which kind of study would you employ?
   a. An adoption study
   b. A family study
   c. Twin studies
   d. Prevalence
   e. All of the above

   Answer: a   p. 440

59. To determine if chromosome _____ was related to schizophrenia, researchers conducted _____ analysis
   a. 22; linkage
   b. 22; genetic
   c. 34; hereditary
   d. 34; dopamine
   e. none of the above

   Answer: a   p. 440

60. There is some evidence that _____ can cause schizophrenia.
   a. deficits in functioning
   b. neurological complications
   c. complications to the fetus during pregnancy
   d. maternal substance use
   e. none of the above

   Answer: c   p. 442

61. Biological theorists explain schizophrenia in terms of _____ amounts of _____.
   a. deficient; dopamine
   b. deficient; norepinephrine
   c. excessive; dopamine
   d. excessive; norepinephrine
   e. fluctuating; norepinephrine

   Answer: c   p. 447

62. Large doses of _____ create a condition indistinguishable from acute paranoid schizophrenia.
   a. alcohol
   b. amphetamine
   c. caffeine
   d. heroin
   e. nicotine

   Answer: b   p. 448

63. Drugs that treat symptoms of schizophrenia also treat
    a. alcoholism.
    b. amphetamine psychosis.
    c. heroin addiction.
    d. Huntington's disease.
    e. Parkinson's disease.

    Answer: b   p. 449

64. If the dopamine hypothesis is correct, we would expect that it would be impossible for
    a. someone to have both schizophrenia and Parkinson's disease.
    b. someone not to have both schizophrenia and Parkinson's disease.
    c. someone to have both depression and schizophrenia.
    d. someone not to have both depression and schizophrenia.
    e. none of the above.

    Answer: a   p. 449

65. Autopsies of the brains of schizophrenic individuals show _____ dopamine receptors.
    a. an increased number of
    b. larger
    c. more efficient
    d. decreased number of
    e. none of the above

    Answer: a   p. 449

66. Abnormalities in brain structure appear to characterize
    a. Type I schizophrenia.
    b. Type II schizophrenia.
    c. paranoid schizophrenia.
    d. disorganized schizophrenia.
    e. none of the above.

    Answer: b   p. 450

67. Research on schizophrenia has found that the _____ is (are) large in people diagnosed with schizophrenia than in those not diagnosed with schizophrenia.
    a. hippocampus
    b. medulla oblongata
    c. limbic system
    d. frontal lobes
    e. ventricles

    Answer: e   p. 451

68. Theorists who locate the origins of schizophrenia within families focus on patterns of
    a. affluence.
    b. communication.
    c. friendship.
    d. influence.
    e. sex-role differentiation.

    Answer: b   p. 452

69. In diathesis-stress language, theories of the role of expressed emotion in schizophrenia focus on
    a. the diathesis.
    b. the stress.
    c. their interaction.
    d. their absence.
    e. the factor determined by the subtype of schizophrenia.

    Answer: a   p. 452

70. The relationship between social class and schizophrenia is _____ in large cities and _____ in small cities.
    a. negative; negative
    b. negative; positive
    c. negative; zero
    d. positive; negative
    e. positive; zero

    Answer: c   p. 453

71. Schizophrenia is overrepresented in the lower social classes. Which of the following theories seems to best explain this finding?
    a. Social mobility hypothesis
    b. Social drift hypothesis
    c. Social causation hypothesis
    d. Social indifference hypothesis
    e. None of the above

    Answer: b   p. 453

72. Research suggests that schizophrenia is
    a. a response to a stressful environment in those with a predisposition to schizophrenia.
    b. a completely genetically determined disorder.
    c. a completely healthy response to stress.
    d. a psychosomatic disorder.
    e. manufactured by society.

    Answer: a   p. 456

73. The major tranquilizers first became available as a treatment for schizophrenia in the
    a. 1930s.
    b. 1940s.
    c. 1950s.
    d. 1960s.
    e. 1970s.

    Answer: c   p. 456

74. We might expect schizophrenic symptoms to be lowest among those who are being treated for
    a. AIDS.
    b. cancer.
    c. hay fever.
    d. gender identity disorder.
    e. warts.

    Answer: c   p. 456

75. Which type of symptoms would major tranquilizers be most likely to affect?
    a. Catatonic
    b. Disorganized
    c. Paranoid
    d. Residual
    e. Undifferentiated

    Answer: c   p. 457

76. Neuroleptics work by
    a. blocking dopamine receptors.
    b. breaking down dopamine.
    c. catalyzing dopamine inhibition.
    d. increasing reuptake of dopamine.
    e. slowing down production of dopamine.

    Answer: a   p. 457

77. All of these are side effects of chlorpromazine *except*
    a. depression.
    b. diarrhea.
    c. drowsiness.
    d. dry mouth.
    e. none of the above.

    Answer: b   p. 457

78. All of the following can be said of tardive dyskinesia *except* that it
    a. involves unusual mouth movement.
    b. is irreversible.
    c. improves with age.
    d. affects up to a quarter of treated schizophrenic patients.
    e. is a side effect of antipsychotic medication.

    Answer: c   p. 458

79. The advent of atypical antipsychotic medication is associated with all of these *except*
    a. a decrease in tardive dyskinesia.
    b. an increase in readmissions.
    c. a decline in hospital populations.
    d. a decrease in psychotic symptoms among those treated.
    e. none of the above.

    Answer: a   p. 458

80. The rate of relapse of schizophrenic patients may be increased by all of these *except*
    a. how much time the patient spends at home.
    b. poor compliance with medications.
    c. hostile emotional quality of home.
    d. low level of work and social skills.
    e. none of the above.

    Answer: e   p. 460

81. Research on a new treatment, _____, has had a positive and encouraging impact on schizophrenia.
    a. psychogenesis
    b. psychoanalysis
    c. strict behavioral management
    d. gestalt therapy
    e. cognitive rehabilitation

    Answer: e   p. 462

CHAPTER 11 | Late-Onset Disorders

1. Advances in medical technologies have extended the life span of humans, thus necessitating
   a. the study of development and the development of mental illness throughout life.
   b. the elimination of certain diagnostic categories in the DSM-IV.
   c. the expansion of therapeutic research to prodromal syndromes in adulthood.
   d. the inclusion of the elderly in certain research studies.
   e. none of the above.

   Answer: a   p. 469

2. Psychological disorders
   a. never develop in the elderly.
   b. can have childhood or elderly onsets.
   c. are more likely to develop in the elderly than in children.
   d. are often less debilitating when onset occurs in the later years of life.
   e. none of the above.

   Answer: b   p. 470

3. There are three identified sources of bias in estimates of mental illness in the elderly. Which of the following is *not* one of those biases?
   a. Misattribution of psychiatric symptoms to cognitive problems
   b. Lack of age-appropriate diagnostic criteria
   c. Underreporting of mental illness because of cognitive deficits
   d. Misattribution of psychiatric symptoms to normal aging
   e. None of the above

   Answer: e   p. 471

4. One of the factors that may lead to the loss of abilities that occur with advanced age is
   a. changes in hormone levels.
   b. abnormal increases in prefrontal activity.
   c. loss of visio-motor functioning.
   d. physical limitations that accompany advancing age.
   e. lack of continued stimulation throughout life.

   Answer: a   p. 473

5. The reason that IQ scores are generally lower in the elderly is
   a. poor test construction.
   b. declines in the ability to store new information.
   c. poor test administration.
   d. lack of research to identify neuoradaptation in the elderly.
   e. retirement.

   Answer: b   p. 474

6. One facet of intelligence that does not seem to change with age is
   a. vocabulary.
   b. mathematical reasoning.
   c. memory.
   d. encoding new information.
   e. processing speed.

   Answer: a   p. 474

7. There is evidence supporting a(n) _____ in diathesis over an individual's lifetime.
   a. increase
   b. stabilization
   c. decrease
   d. nonlinear progression
   e. an initial increase then stabilization, and then another increase

   Answer: c   p. 475

8. There is evidence supporting a(n) _____ in biological vulnerability over an individual's lifetime.
   a. increase
   b. stabilization
   c. decrease
   d. nonlinear progression
   e. an initial increase then stabilization, and then another increase

   Answer: a   p. 475

9. The general, progressive deterioration of cognitive functioning that is often accompanied by changes in psychological and emotional states is called
   a. aphasia.
   b. apraxia.
   c. dementia.
   d. Alzheimer's disease.
   e. Parkinson's disease.

   Answer: c   p. 475

10. The deterioration in the ability to communicate with language is called
    a. aphasia.
    b. apraxia.
    c. dementia.
    d. Alzheimer's disease.
    e. Parkinson's disease.

    Answer: a   p. 475

11. The manifested decline in motor skills is called
    a. aphasia.
    b. apraxia.
    c. dementia.
    d. Alzheimer's disease.
    e. Parkinson's disease.

    Answer: b   p. 475

12. The failure to identify familiar objects or faces is called
    a. agnosia.
    b. apraxia.
    c. dementia.
    d. Alzheimer's disease.
    e. Parkinson's disease.

    Answer: a   p. 476

13. Individuals experiencing any form of dementia are also likely to be suffering from
    a. depression.
    b. psychosis.
    c. a personality disorder.
    d. all of the above.
    e. a and b.

    Answer: e   p. 477

14. Betty is picked up and brought to the emergency room because she was wandering the streets, not able to find her home or to remember her phone number. The hospital staff begins to consider that Betty may be suffering from
    a. substance abuse.
    b. apraxia.
    c. dementia.
    d. Alzheimer's disease.
    e. Any of the above.

    Answer: e   p. 47

15. The development of cognitive impairment and multiple cognitive deficits manifested by memory impairment, cognitive disturbances, without comorbid substance use, could be
    a. aphasia.
    b. apraxia.
    c. dementia.
    d. Alzheimer's disease.
    e. Parkinson's disease.

    Answer: d   p. 477

16. At least _____ of those diagnosed with dementia may have Alzheimer's disease.
    a. 25 percent
    b. 35 percent
    c. 50 percent
    d. 65 percent
    e. 75 percent

    Answer: c   p. 477

17. The most frequent cause of dementia is
    a. AIDS.
    b. Alzheimer's disease.
    c. Huntington's chorea.
    d. Korsakoff's syndrome.
    e. Parkinson's disease.

    Answer: b   p. 477

18. For which of the following disorders are women at higher risk than men?
    a. AIDS
    b. Alzheimer's disease
    c. Huntington's chorea
    d. Korsakoff's syndrome
    e. Parkinson's disease

    Answer: b   p. 477

19. Which of these statements about Alzheimer's disease is *false?*
    a. Age influences onset.
    b. The disease is hereditary.
    c. Onset is sudden.
    d. There is an associated pathology of biochemistry.
    e. There is an associated pathology of brain structure.

    Answer: c   p. 478

20. If you were assessing a demented patient and you found evidence of senile plaques, you would consider a diagnosis of
    a. AIDS dementia complex.
    b. Pick's disease.
    c. Alzheimer's disease.
    d. Korsakoff's syndrome.
    e. Parkinson's disease.

    Answer: c   p. 479

21. One theory about the cause of Alzheimer's disease attributes it to an increased amount of _____ in the body.
    a. alcohol
    b. aluminum
    c. dopamine
    d. vitamin B
    e. zinc

    Answer: b   p. 479

22. One theory about the cause of Alzheimer's disease links it to an enzyme deficit resulting in a deficiency of
    a. dopamine.
    b. norepinephrine.
    c. serotonin.
    d. acetylcholine.
    e. epinephrine.

    Answer: d   p. 480

23. One theory about the cause of Alzheimer's disease links it to chromosomal abnormalities related to those responsible for
    a. alcoholism.
    b. bipolar depression.
    c. color blindness.
    d. Down syndrome.
    e. hemophilia.

    Answer: d   p. 480

24. Current treatments for Alzheimer's disease include all of the following *except*
    a. nicotine.
    b. estrogen.
    c. nonsteroidal anti-inflammatory drugs.
    d. acetylcholine.
    e. none of the above.

    Answer: e   p. 482

25. The primary cause of vascular dementia is
    a. stroke.
    b. heart disease.
    c. plaques.
    d. tangles.
    e. lack of acetylcholine.

    Answer: a   p. 483

26. Vascular dementia can result in
    a. memory confabulation.
    b. areas of dying or dead brain tissue.
    c. plaques.
    d. tangles.
    e. none of the above.

    Answer: b   p. 483

27. Of the following which has the most severe impact on psychological functioning?
    a. Alzheimer's disease
    b. Parkinson's disease
    c. vascular dementia
    d. frontal lobe dementia
    e. Huntington's disease

    Answer: c   p. 484

28. Pick's disease is also known as
    a. Alzheimer's disease.
    b. Parkinson's disease.
    c. vascular dementia.
    d. frontal lobe dementia.
    e. Huntington's disease.

    Answer: d   p. 485

29. Which the following is marked by significant changes in personality?
    a. Alzheimer's disease
    b. Parkinson's disease
    c. vascular dementia
    d. frontal lobe dementia
    e. Huntington's disease

    Answer: d   p. 484

30. A disorder that is a result of degeneration of dopamine neurons is called
    a. Alzheimer's disease.
    b. Parkinson's disease.
    c. vascular dementia.
    d. frontal lobe dementia.
    e. Huntington's disease.

    Answer: b   p. 484

31. Individuals who suffer from Parkinson's induced dementia are more likely to have come from a family with a history of _____ than those with Parkinson's disease but not Parkinson's induced dementia.
    a. Alzheimer's disease
    b. vascular dementia
    c. frontal lobe dementia
    d. Huntington's disease
    e. None of the above

    Answer: a   p. 486

32. Probably the easiest methods for identifying which type of dementia an elderly individual is suffering from is
    a. to do a complete neurological exam.
    b. to do a postmortem autopsy of the brain.
    c. to prescribe different medications until you find the one that works.
    d. to use neuroimaging.
    e. none of the above.

    Answer: b   p. 486

33. A disorder that has a rapid onset, fluctuates over time, and usually responds rapidly to treatment is
    a. Alzheimer's disease.
    b. Parkinson's disease.
    c. vascular dementia.
    d. frontal lobe dementia.
    e. delirium.

    Answer: e   p. 484

34. When a patient presents with what appears to be delirium, it is important to differentiate between
    a. delirium and Alzheimer's disease.
    b. Parkinson's disease and delirium.
    c. vascular dementia and delirium.
    d. substance induced delirium and delirium.
    e. frontal lobe dementia and delirium.

    Answer: d   p. 484

35. While people over the age of _____ shows the least amount of depression, there appears to be a sharp increase in depression after the age of _____.
    a. 45; 65
    b. 65; 80
    c. 25; 80
    d. 40; 80
    e. 20; 65

    Answer: b   p. 489

36. You are a clinician working on a geriatric ward. A new patient comes in who is suffering from late-life depression. When considering treatments for this patient, you remember that late-life depression should be
    a. treated differently than depression is treated in younger adults.
    b. treated differently than depression is treated in children.
    c. treated in the same manner that depression is treated in younger individuals.
    d. not treated at all, as it might be temporary, related to a family member's or friend's death.
    e. none of the above.

    Answer: c   p. 490

37. Another disorder that is quite prevalent in young individuals but seems to decline with age is
    a. anxiety.
    b. dementia.
    c. adjustment disorder.
    d. substance abuse.
    e. a and d.

    Answer: a   p. 492

38. The substance(s) most commonly abused by the elderly is (are)
    a. cocaine.
    b. marijuana.
    c. heroin.
    d. prescription medications.
    e. alcohol.

    Answer: e   p. 493

39. If a person comes to see you and is suffering from nonbizzare delusions, you could diagnose a delusional disorder. However, you must first
    a. rule out medical conditions.
    b. make sure that they have never met criteria for schizophrenia.
    c. determine they are not a result of substance use.
    d. determine there is no evidence of a mood disorder.
    e. all of the above.

    Answer: e   p. 495

40. Late-onset schizophrenia is
    a. also called paraphrenia.
    b. more prevalent in women than men.
    c. treated in the same manner that schizophrenia in younger individuals is treated.
    d. marked with social isolation.
    e. all of the above.

    Answer: e   p. 497

CHAPTER 12

Psychological Factors and Physical Disorders

1. Diathesis-stress models are compatible with _____ approaches.
   a. biological
   b. environmental
   c. mental
   d. all of the above
   e. a and b

   Answer: a   p. 504

2. Diathesis refers to a(n)
   a. constitutional weakness.
   b. environmental trigger.
   c. family member with a psychological disorder.
   d. traumatic event in childhood.
   e. unconscious conflict.

   Answer: a   p. 504

3. The discussion of biological mechanisms that are affected by psychological factors focuses primarily on the
   a. HPA axis.
   b. limbic system.
   c. frontal lobe.
   d. immune system.
   e. both a and d

   Answer: e   p. 504

149

4. Selye's general adaptation syndrome is
   a. disease specific.
   b. organ specific.
   c. species specific.
   d. syndrome specific.
   e. none of the above.

   Answer: e   p. 505

5. What is the correct sequence in the general adaptation syndrome?
   a. Alarm → countershock → resistance → exhaustion
   b. Countershock → alarm → exhaustion → resistance
   c. Countershock → resistance → exhaustion → alarm
   d. Exhaustion → alarm → countershock → resistance
   e. Alarm → resistance → exhaustion → countershock

   Answer: a   p. 506

6. According to the stages of Selye's general adaptation syndrome, if you were to develop the flu during finals week, it could indicate
   a. a failure of the alarm reaction.
   b. that you have entered the exhaustion stage.
   c. that you never achieved the resistance stage.
   d. all of the above.
   e. a and b.

   Answer: d   p. 506

7. The stable internal balance of bodily systems is called
   a. allostasis.
   b. homeostasis.
   c. alogia.
   d. heterogeneity.
   e. homogeneity.

   Answer: b   p. 506

8. The adaptation of bodily states simultaneously across many different life circumstances to maintain stability is called
   a. allostasis.
   b. homeostasis.
   c. alogia.
   d. heterogeneity.
   e. homogeneity.

   Answer: a   p. 507

9. Which of the following does *not* occur when the body experiences stress?
   a. Activation of the sympathetic nervous system
   b. Release of certain hormones in the brain
   c. Release of certain hormones in the body
   d. Activation of the psychoneuroimmunological system
   e. Activation of the hypothalamus

   Answer: d   p. 507

10. A man goes to see a doctor complaining of chest pain. He describes his lifestyle as highly stressful, stating that he works at a job were he is often stressed and has little control. He also states that he has been told by other doctors that he has high blood pressure. The doctor could assume that this man may be at risk for developing
   a. a somatoform disorder.
   b. coronary heart disease.
   c. psychogenic fugue.
   d. allostasis.
   e. adrenal gland dysfunction.

   Answer: b   p. 507

11. The study of how psychological factors change neural activity in the immune system is called
   a. psychoneuroimmunology.
   b. immunoneurology.
   c. immunopsychology.
   d. health psychology.
   e. none of the above.

   Answer: a   p. 509

12. Holmes and Rahe found that as the number of stressful life events increases, so too does
   a. illness.
   b. depression.
   c. injuries.
   d. a and b.
   e. none of the above.

   Answer: d   p. 511

13. Which of the following is considered the most stressful life event?
   a. Divorce
   b. Job loss
   c. Retirement
   d. Personal injury
   e. Death of a spouse

   Answer: e   p. 512

14. When events are _____, they are most likely to lead to illness.
    a. controllable
    b. uncontrollable
    c. only moderately controllable
    d. controllable but unpredictable
    e. predictable but uncontrollable

    Answer: b   p. 512

15. According to Holmes and Rahe, which would *not* be stressful?
    a. Developing cancer
    b. Winning an award
    c. Going away with the family
    d. Being convicted of a felony
    e. None of the above

    Answer: e   p. 512

16. In the language of the diathesis-stress model, Holmes and Rahe studied the _____ and Selye studied the _____.
    a. diathesis; diathesis
    b. diathesis; stress
    c. stress; diathesis
    d. stress; stress
    e. none of the above

    Answer: d   p. 513

17. _____ likely plays a role in the development of psychosomatic disorders.
    a. Coronary heart disease
    b. Classical conditioning
    c. Operant conditioning
    d. Immunodysfunction
    e. Unresolved conflicts in the unconscious

    Answer: b   p. 514

18. Which of these is *not* a risk factor for coronary heart disease?
    a. Low serum cholesterol
    b. Growing old
    c. High blood pressure
    d. Physical inactivity
    e. Smoking cigarettes

    Answer: a   p. 515

19. Type A coronary prone behavior is characterized by all of these *except*
    a. initial helplessness in the face of frustration.
    b. ambition.
    c. competitiveness.
    d. hostility.
    e. time urgency.

    Answer: a   p. 515

20. Longitudinal studies of the population at large suggested that people with
    Type A personality have about _____ times the risk of experiencing
    coronary heart disease as people with Type B personality.
    a. 2
    b. 5
    c. 25
    d. 50
    e. 100

    Answer: a   p. 516

21. The text describes studies showing that the opportunity to vent hostility
    _____ your blood pressure.
    a. does not affect
    b. lowers
    c. raises
    d. dysregulates
    e. hyperregulates

    Answer: b   p. 517

22. When researchers decompose the elements of Type A coronary prone
    behavior, they find that _____ is the critical ingredient that predicts
    subsequent coronary heart disease.
    a. ambition
    b. competitiveness
    c. hostility
    d. physical inactivity
    e. time urgency

    Answer: c   p. 517

23. David Glass conceives Type A coronary prone behavior as a lifelong
    struggle to _____ the world.
    a. accommodate
    b. assimilate
    c. control
    d. predict
    e. understand

    Answer: c   p. 518

24. David Glass proposes that when people who show Type A coronary prone behavior fail to control events in the world, they respond with
    a. denial.
    b. humor.
    c. anger.
    d. profound helplessness.
    e. renewed effort.

    Answer: d   p. 518

25. A study of Harvard students found that the need for _____, when _____, predicted high blood pressure decades later.
    a. achievement; excited
    b. achievement; inhibited
    c. affiliation; inhibited
    d. power; excited
    e. power; inhibited

    Answer: e   p. 518

26. In a study of victims of a first heart attack, which was the best predictor of death from a second heart attack?
    a. Pessimism
    b. Helplessness
    c. Type A personality
    d. Damage to the heart from the first heart attack
    e. Traditional physical risk factors

    Answer: a   p. 519

27. The text integrates findings on Type A behavior, coronary heart disease, and hypertension with the simple assumption that
    a. coronary fitness is solely determined by genetics.
    b. hypertension is the underlying cause of Type A behavior and coronary heart disease.
    c. the heart has only a fixed number of beats allotted.
    d. Type A behavior is the underlying cause of coronary heart disease and hypertension.
    e. Type A behavior, hypertension, and coronary heart disease fall along a continuum.

    Answer: c   p. 519

28. Work puts a strain on the heart that is reflected in coronary heart disease when the work involves
    a. high choice.
    b. high demand.
    c. low choice.
    d. a and b.
    e. b and c.

    Answer: e   p. 520

29. According to the text, the long-term effect of vigorous exercise is to
    _____ the heart
    a. challenge
    b. conserve
    c. exhaust
    d. stress
    e. none of the above

    Answer: b   p. 521

30. An erosion of the mucous membrane, or peptic ulcer, can occur in
    a. the stomach.
    b. the small intestine.
    c. the duodenum.
    d. all of the above.
    e. b and c.

    Answer: d   p. 521

31. About _____ people in the United States today have peptic ulcers.
    a. 100,000
    b. 250,000
    c. 1 million
    d. 10 million
    e. 25 million

    Answer: e   p. 522

32. Ulcer pain usually occurs
    a. after eating.
    b. before eating.
    c. during eating.
    d. constantly.
    e. off and on, with no particular pattern.

    Answer: a   p. 522

33. Ulcer pain is usually felt in the
    a. small of the back.
    b. legs.
    c. abdomen.
    d. kidneys.
    e. chest.

    Answer: c   p. 522

34. The stomach is protected from digestive juices by
    a. HCl acid.
    b. mucous.
    c. pepsin.
    d. presence of food.
    e. rapid digestion.

    Answer: b   p. 523

35. The diathesis in ulcer development may be any of the following *except*
    a. a slowly regenerating stomach lining.
    b. excess stomach acid secretion.
    c. the effects of disturbing events in the environment.
    d. a weak mucous coating.
    e. none of the above.

    Answer: c   p. 523

36. Peptic ulcers are most common among _____ class individuals.
    a. lower
    b. middle
    c. upper
    d. top-most
    e. There are no social class differences.

    Answer: a   p. 523

37. Emotional states like anxiety and anger _____ stomach acid, and states like depression and helplessness _____ stomach acid.
    a. increase; increase
    b. increase; decrease
    c. decrease; increase
    d. decrease; decrease
    e. increase; do not affect

    Answer: b   p. 524

38. The notion that individuals in certain professions tend to have more ulcers is
    a. false.
    b. true, and the direction of causality runs from the job to the ulcer.
    c. true, and the direction of causality runs from the ulcer to the job.
    d. true, but the direction of causality is unclear.
    e. not yet known.

    Answer: d   p. 524

39. Research with animals shows that all of the following situations can produce ulcers *except*
    a. approach-avoidance conflicts.
    b. signaled aversive events.
    c. uncontrollable aversive events.
    d. unpredictable bad events.
    e. none of the above.

    Answer: b   p. 525

40. Research on rats revealed that
    a. controllability and predictability cause ulcers.
    b. controllability makes ulcers likely but predictability does not play a role in the cause of ulcers.
    c. controllability and unpredictability cause ulcers.
    d. lack of control and unpredictability make ulcers more likely.
    e. lack of control makes it likely predictability does not play a role in the cause of ulcers.

    Answer: d   p. 525

41. The treatment of choice for ulcer patients is
    a. antacids.
    b. antidepressants.
    c. cimetidine.
    d. surgery.
    e. tranquilizers.

    Answer: c   p. 526

42. Currently, the best available treatment of ulcers addresses the
    a. diathesis.
    b. stress.
    c. symptoms.
    d. a and b.
    e. none of the above.

    Answer: c   p. 526

43. The text concludes that ulcers are best explained in _____ terms.
    a. behavioral
    b. biological
    c. cognitive
    d. diathesis-stress
    e. psychodynamic

    Answer: d   p. 526

44. The text argues that hopelessness is involved in which of the following?
    a. Asthma
    b. Death following stroke
    c. Death during bereavement
    d. Influenza
    e. b and c

    Answer: e   p. 527

45 Research has linked pessimistic explanatory style to which of the following?
    a. Early death
    b. Infectious illness
    c. Lowered immunocompetence
    d. Number of doctor visits
    e. All of the above

    Answer: e   p. 528

46. The text describes research looking at the relations among explanatory style, immunocompetence, illness, and death. Which link is *not* proposed?
    a. Depression → endorphins
    b. Lowered immune function → pessimism
    c. Endorphins → lowered immune function
    d. Lowered immune function → tumors
    e. Pessimism → depression

    Answer: b   p. 528

47. Psychological factors can _____ and _____ the HIV virus.
    a. influence; be influenced by
    b. worsen; influence
    c. treat; be influenced by
    d. be influenced by; worsen
    e. none of the above

    Answer: a   p. 528

48. Recent research has found that psychotherapy for cancer patients can
    a. stop cancer spread.
    b. increase cancer spread.
    c. decrease survival time.
    d. increase survival time.
    e. all of the above.

    Answer: d   p. 530

49. According to the text, psychological factors exacerbate asthma in
    a. all children.
    b. some children but not others.
    c. no children.
    d. Research is contradictory.
    e. Research has not yet been conducted.

    Answer: b   p. 531

50. Asthma attacks may
    a. be caused by family interactions.
    b. be factors in the ability to control the disease.
    c. occur only when the body is exerting itself.
    d. be linked to substance use.
    e. all of the above.

    Answer: a   p. 532

CHAPTER 13 | Sexual Disorders

1. Attitudes about sexuality have changed
   a. surprisingly little over time.
   b. somewhat over time.
   c. considerably over time and place.
   d. but frequency of sexual behavior has not.
   e. but types of behavior engaged in have not.

   Answer: c   p. 535

2. Which of these is *not* described as a layer of erotic life in the text?
   a. Gender identity
   b. Sexual interest
   c. Sexual orientation
   d. Sexual preoccupation
   e. Sex role

   Answer: d   p. 536

3. According to the text, gender identity refers to the
   a. sexual objects you find erotic.
   b. gender you are attracted to.
   c. gender you feel you are.
   d. way you engage in sex.
   e. gender you behave like.

   Answer: c   p. 536

4. According to the text, sexual orientation refers to the
   a. sexual objects you find erotic.
   b. gender you are attracted to.
   c. gender you feel you are.
   d. way you engage in sex.
   e. gender you behave like.

   Answer: b   p. 536

5. According to the text, sexual interest refers to the
   a. sexual objects you find erotic.
   b. gender you are attracted to.
   c. gender you feel you are.
   d. way you engage in sex.
   e. gender you behave like.

   Answer: a   p. 536

6. Which sexual layer does *not* have a defined category of disorders associated with it?
   a. Sexual identity
   b. Sexual interest
   c. Sexual orientation
   d. Sexual performance
   e. Sex role

   Answer: e   p. 537

7. According to the text, sexual performance refers to the
   a. sexual objects you find erotic.
   b. gender you are attracted to.
   c. gender you feel you are.
   d. sexual functioning.
   e. gender you behave like.

   Answer: d   p. 537

8. Transsexualism is a problem with
   a. androgyny.
   b. gender identity.
   c. sex role.
   d. sexual function.
   e. sexual object choice.

   Answer: b   p. 537

9. Transsexuals _____ find cross-dressing sexually arousing.
   a. do
   b. sometimes
   c. do not
   d. initially but not eventually
   e. eventually but not initially

   Answer: c   p. 537

10. Consider a preoperative transsexual who has female genitals. This individual is sexually attracted to females. From the viewpoint of this individual, this sexual preference is
   a. ambiguous.
   b. bisexual.
   c. heterosexual.
   d. homosexual.
   e. transsexual.

   Answer: c   p. 538

11. The frequency of (genetically) male to (genetically) female transsexuals is
   a. between 1 to 10 and 3 to 10.
   b. between 1 to 2 and 1 to 1.
   c. 1 to 1.
   d. between 1 to 1 and 2 to 1.
   e. between 2 to 1 and 6 to 1.

   Answer: e   p. 538

12. People who have androgen insensitivity syndrome are
   a. born genetically male.
   b. born genetically female.
   c. females who have elevated levels of testosterone.
   d. males who have high levels of testosterone.
   e. none of the above.

   Answer: a   p. 539

13. Adrenogenital syndrome
   a. bathes a female fetus in male hormones creating male genitalia.
   b. bathes a male fetus in female hormones creating female genitalia.
   c. is chromosomally represented as XY.
   d. Is chromosomally represented as XX.
   e. a and d.

   Answer: e   p. 540

14. The treatment for gender identity disorder is to change
    a. attitudes toward the self.
    b. sexual identity.
    c. society.
    d. the body.
    e. none of the above.

    Answer: d   p. 542

15. _____ operations to treat transsexualism are more difficult because
    _____.
    a. Male-to-female; the surgery is more complicated
    b. Male-to-female; patients begin with more psychological difficulties
    c. Female-to-male; the surgery is more complicated
    d. Female-to-male; patients begin with more psychological difficulties
    e. Repeated; insurance policies only cover the first operation

    Answer: c   p. 543

16. According to the text, sexual orientation refers to the
    a. sexual objects you find erotic.
    b. gender you are attracted to.
    c. gender you feel you are.
    d. way you engage in sex.
    e. gender you behave like.

    Answer: b   p. 543

17. Current studies imply that sexual orientation is fundamentally due to
    a. chance.
    b. fetal hormones.
    c. genetics.
    d. social learning.
    e. unresolved unconscious conflicts.

    Answer: b   p. 544

18. One theory of the origin of homosexuality described in the text links it to
    anatomical brain differences. What prediction *cannot* be made from this
    theory?
    a. Neuroanatomic features of homosexual brains lie somewhere between
       heterosexual males and females.
    b. Homosexuality is more common among males than females.
    c. Homosexuality is unalterable.
    d. Stereotypes that male homosexuals are effeminate are correct.
    e. All of the above.

    Answer: b   p. 544

19. Research has shown that identical twins have a higher concordance rate than fraternal twins of being homosexual; this suggests
    a. that there is no evidence that genetics play a role in sexual orientation.
    b. that there is evidence that genetics play a role in sexual orientation.
    c. that there is evidence that environment plays a stronger role than genetics in determining sexual orientation.
    d. that sexual orientation is not determined in the womb.
    e. none of the above.

    Answer: b   p. 545

20. Which of these is *no longer* considered a sexual disorder or dysfunction?
    a. Homosexuality
    b. Impotence
    c. Paraphilia
    d. Transsexuality
    e. Transvestism

    Answer: a   p. 545

21. Homosexuality that is a source of distress to the person is termed
    a. ego dystonic.
    b. ego pathogenic.
    c. ego syntonic.
    d. normal.
    e. pathological.

    Answer: a   p. 545

22. _____ can change homosexuality, but chiefly among those with

    _____.
    a. Behavior modification; little homosexual experience
    b. Behavior modification; some heterosexual experience
    c. Psychoanalysis; little homosexual experience
    d. Psychoanalysis; some heterosexual experience
    e. Either psychoanalysis or behavior modification; guilt

    Answer: b   p. 545

23. According to the text, sexual interest refers to the
    a. sexual objects you find erotic.
    b. gender you are attracted to.
    c. gender you feel you are.
    d. way you engage in sex.
    e. gender you behave like.

    Answer: a   p. 546

24. Paraphilic fantasies are considered true paraphilic disorders when
    a. the individual is distressed by his or her actions.
    b. the object becomes necessary for arousal.
    c. the object displaces a human partner.
    d. all of the above.
    e. none of the above.

    Answer: e   p. 546

25. A fetish generally refers to a(n) _____ sexual object choice.
    a. humiliated
    b. illegal
    c. immoral
    d. nonconsenting
    e. nonliving

    Answer: e   p. 546

26. Most people with fetishes are
    a. adolescents of either sex.
    b. adult females.
    c. adult males.
    d. female children.
    e. male children.

    Answer: c   p. 547

27. Transvestism is
    a. any form of cross-dressing.
    b. cross-dressing to attract same sex partners.
    c. cross-dressing as a means of sexual gratification.
    d. illegal cross-dressing.
    e. provocative cross-dressing.

    Answer: c   p. 547

28. Transvestites are typically
    a. homosexual.
    b. transsexual.
    c. heterosexual.
    d. bisexual.
    e. asexual.

    Answer: c   p. 548

29. A person who becomes sexually aroused by inflicting suffering or humiliation on another person is a
   a. sadist.
   b. masochist.
   c. transvestite.
   d. homosexual
   e. sadomasochist.

   Answer: a   p. 549

30. A person who becomes sexually aroused by having suffering or humiliation inflicted on him or her is a
   a. sadist.
   b. masochist.
   c. transvestite.
   d. homosexual
   e. sadomasochist.

   Answer: b   p. 549

31. Sadists are usually _____, and masochists are usually _____.
   a. men; men
   b. men; women
   c. women; men
   d. women; women
   e. men; men or women

   Answer: a   p. 550

32. Which does *not* belong?
   a. Telephone scatologia
   b. Exhibitionism
   c. Masochism
   d. Voyeurism
   e. Pedophilia

   Answer: c   p. 551

33. The most common sexual crime in the United States is
   a. exhibitionism.
   b. pedophilia.
   c. rape.
   d. transvestism.
   e. voyeurism.

   Answer: a   p. 551

34. Telephone scatologia consists of
    a. having a telephone fetish.
    b. abusing pay-for-sex phone numbers.
    c. recurrent and intense sexual urges to make obscene phone calls.
    d. having a masturbatory fantasy while on the phone with a family member.
    e. none of the above.

    Answer: c   p. 551

35. Exhibitionism often involves _____ as its end goal.
    a. the risk of the exposure
    b. sexual intercourse
    c. exciting voyeurs
    d. public masturbation
    e. none of the above

    Answer: a   p. 552

36. According to the text, exhibitionists usually
    a. are unmarried.
    b. are not dangerous.
    c. prefer a particular type of victim.
    d. prefer privacy.
    e. b and c.

    Answer: e   p. 552

37. Which of these characteristics is *not* typical of exhibitionists?
    a. Male
    b. Married
    c. Pedophiliac
    d. Immaturity
    e. All of the above

    Answer: c   p. 552

38. Exhibitionism is a disorder of _____, and voyeurism is a disorder
    of _____.
    a. men; men
    b. men; women
    c. women; men
    d. women; women
    e. men; men or women

    Answer: a   p. 552

39. Exhibitionism is to voyeurism as
    a. male is to female.
    b. young is to old.
    c. public is to private.
    d. sadism is to masochism.
    e. fetish is to paraphilia.

    Answer: c   p. 552

40. A voyeur typically
    a. is married.
    b. approaches his victim for contact.
    c. is aroused by the illegal, secretive nature of his act.
    d. had normal adolescent adjustment.
    e. all of the above.

    Answer: c   p. 553

41. The most heavily punished paraphilia is
    a. exhibitionism.
    b. pedophilia.
    c. rape.
    d. transvestism.
    e. voyeurism.

    Answer: b   p. 553

42. Which of these is *not* a typical characteristic of a pedophile?
    a. Inept at adult relationships
    b. Male
    c. Religious
    d. Single-time offenders
    e. All of the above

    Answer: d   p. 553

43. A sexually molested child usually is all of these *except*
    a. a girl.
    b. known by the molester.
    c. physically beaten.
    d. usually less upset than his or her parents.
    e. all of the above.

    Answer: c   p. 554

44. Relative to a younger pedophile, an older pedophile seeks out
    a. boys.
    b. girls.
    c. older children.
    d. younger children.
    e. none of the above.

    Answer: d   p. 554

45. Psychodynamic theorists describe fetishes as
    a. negative catharses.
    b. negative cathexes.
    c. positive catharses.
    d. positive cathexes.
    e. none of the above.

    Answer: d   p. 554

46. The psychodynamic view of fetishes fails to explain _____; the classical conditioning account of fetishes fails to explain _____.
    a. why it begins in childhood; how the erotic association develops
    b. why it develops in a particular individual; why there is limited class of fetish objects
    c. how the erotic association develops; why it begins in childhood
    d. why there is limited class of fetish objects; why it develops in a particular individual
    e. why a slipper?; why a slipper?

    Answer: b   p. 555

47. The notion of preparedness explains the _____ fetishes.
    a. abnormality of
    b. guilt associated with
    c. popularity of
    d. selectivity of
    e. sex difference in

    Answer: d   p. 555

48. The use of behavior therapy to treat paraphilias meets with _____ success.
    a. absolutely no
    b. little
    c. some
    d. much
    e. total

    Answer: c   p. 555

49. The use of imaginal sexual stimuli followed by aversive unconditioned stimuli is called
    a. aversion therapy.
    b. covert sensitization.
    c. classical conditioning.
    d. cathexis.
    e. none of the above.

    Answer: b   p. 555

50. According to the text, sex role refers to the
    a. sexual objects you find erotic.
    b. sex you are attracted to.
    c. sex you feel you are.
    d. way you engage in sex.
    e. sex you behave like.

    Answer: e   p. 556

51. Androgyny is another word for
    a. homosexuality.
    b. heterosexuality.
    c. bisexuality.
    d. transexuality.
    e. none of the above.

    Answer: e   p. 558

52. According to the text, sexual performance refers to the
    a. sexual objects you find erotic.
    b. sex you are attracted to.
    c. sex you feel you are.
    d. way you engage in sex.
    e. sex you behave like.

    Answer: d   p. 559

53. What is the correct chronological order?
    a. Erotic desire → physical excitement → orgasm → resolution
    b. Physical excitement → orgasm → arousal → resolution
    c. Arousal → excitement → resolution
    d. Erotic desire → excitement → arousal → resolution
    e. Any of the above, depending on the person

    Answer: a   p. 559

54. In males, erection is controlled by the _____ nervous system, and orgasm is controlled by the _____ nervous system.
    a. parasympathetic; parasympathetic
    b. parasympathetic; sympathetic
    c. sympathetic; parasympathetic
    d. sympathetic; sympathetic
    e. unsympathetic; unsympathetic

    Answer: b   p. 559

55. Only men experience
    a. desire.
    b. arousal.
    c. excitement.
    d. orgasm.
    e. refractory period.

    Answer: e   p. 560

56. Sexual dysfunctions occur with regard to
    a. desire.
    b. arousal.
    c. excitement.
    d. orgasm.
    e. all of the above

    Answer: e   p. 560

57. When a woman experiences a lack of sexual desire and impairment, she is said to be suffering from
    a. sexual unresponsiveness.
    b. sexual aversion disorder.
    c. an orgasmic disorder.
    d. a sexual pain disorder.
    e. dysapreunia.

    Answer: b   p. 561

58. The difference between primary and secondary sexual dysfunction refers to the _____ of the problem.
    a. cause
    b. history
    c. pervasiveness
    d. prognosis
    e. psychological consequences

    Answer: b   p. 562

59. Negative emotions can affect sexuality through
    a. exciting autonomic arousal.
    b. inhibiting autonomic arousal.
    c. bypassing autonomic arousal.
    d. negative emotions do not affect sexuality.
    e. exciting adrenal glands prematurely.

    Answer: b   p. 566

60. Brief sex therapy reportedly fails _____ of the time.
    a. 1 percent
    b. 5 percent
    c. 10 percent
    d. 25 percent
    e. 50 percent

    Answer: d   p. 567

61. Which of these is *not* part of Masters and Johnson's direct sex therapy?
    a. Decreasing anxiety
    b. Explicit instruction in sexual behavior
    c. Regarding problems as neuroses
    d. Treating couples
    e. All of the above

    Answer: c   p. 567

62. Sensate focus is a _____ technique.
    a. behavioral
    b. biological
    c. cognitive
    d. community
    e. psychoanalytic

    Answer: a   p. 568

63. Masters and Johnson's work applies to sexual
    a. definitions.
    b. deviations.
    c. discriminations.
    d. disorders.
    e. dysfunctions.

    Answer: e   p. 568

64. Newer and more popular treatments for sexual dysfunction are
    a. pharmacological treatments.
    b. sensate focus techniques.
    c. in-home therapy.
    d. surgeries.
    e. none of the above.

    Answer: a   p. 569

CHAPTER 14 | Substance-Use Disorders

1. Which of the following is *not* suggested by the text as a reason for using and abusing substances?
   a. Improving mood
   b. Causing euphoria
   c. Altering perception
   d. Reducing anxiety
   e. All of the above

   Answer: e   p. 575

2. The leading health problem in the United States today is
   a. AIDS.
   b. cancer.
   c. heart disease.
   d. substance abuse.
   e. toxic waste.

   Answer: d   p. 576

3. Although the interpretations of substance abuse have changed over the years, the model that has had the most influence in this century has been the
   a. medical disease model.
   b. criminal model.
   c. psychological model.
   d. social deficits model.
   e. social drift model.

   Answer: a   p. 577

4. In the DSM-IV, which of the following is necessary for a diagnosis of substance dependence?
   a. Loss of control regarding drug use
   b. A great deal of time spent trying to acquire the drug
   c. Experiencing withdrawal when the substance is removed
   d. Development of tolerance to the drug
   e. All of the above

   Answer: e   p. 578

5. In the DSM-IV, which of the following is necessary for a diagnosis of substance abuse?
   a. Loss of control regarding drug use
   b. Continued use despite negative consequences
   c. Compulsive use of the drug
   d. Substance dependence
   e. All of the above

   Answer: b   p. 578

6. A cluster of physiological, behavioral, and cognitive phenomena in which the use of a substance or class of substances takes on a much higher priority for a given individual then other behaviors that once held higher value is called
   a. neuroadaptation.
   b. substance dependence.
   c. dependence syndrome.
   d. substance abuse.
   e. drug abuse.

   Answer: c   p. 579

7. The concept in which the constant presence of the drug somehow induces long-lasting changes in the brain is called
   a. neuroadaptation.
   b. substance dependence.
   c. dependence syndrome.
   d. substance abuse.
   e. neuroplasticity.

   Answer: a   p. 579

8. Which of the following determines the potency of a drug?
   a. The route of administration
   b. The ability of the drug to enter the brain
   c. How well the drug interacts with receptors in the brain
   d. How quickly the body and brain adapt to the drug
   e. All of the above

   Answer: e   p. 580

9. The street jargon term for intravenous drug injection is
   a. *chipping.*
   b. *popping.*
   c. *snorting.*
   d. *mainlining.*
   e. *dropping.*

   Answer: d   p. 580

10. Which of the following routes of administration reaches the brain the fastest?
    a. Injected
    b. Oral
    c. Smoked
    d. Sniffed
    e. All are equal.

    Answer: a   p. 580

11. Which of the following may inhibit drug compounds from entering the circulatory system?
    a. Neuroadaptation
    b. Lipid solubility
    c. Blood-brain barrier
    d. Tolerance
    e. All of the above

    Answer: b   p. 582

12. Tolerance is indicated by which of these?
    a. Requiring the drug for normal functioning
    b. Observable physical signs on cessation of use
    c. A decreased response to a drug following repeated use
    d. Amount of time using the drug
    e. Amount of the drug used each time

    Answer: c   p. 582

13. Physical dependence is indicated by which of these?
    a. Requiring the drug for normal functioning
    b. Observable physical signs upon cessation of use
    c. A decreased response to a drug following repeated use
    d. Neuroadaptation
    e. All of the above

    Answer: d   p. 582

14. A withdrawal syndrome is indicated by which of these?
    a. Requiring the drug for normal functioning
    b. Observable physical signs on cessation of use
    c. A decreased response to a drug following repeated use
    d. Evidence that neuroadaptation has occurred
    e. Evidence of tolerance

    Answer: b   p. 583

15. A patient who has had numerous operations and has received narcotics continually following a motor vehicle accident complains of depression and irritability every time his dose of narcotic is reduced. The problem he is experiencing is best described as
    a. neuroadaptation.
    b. tolerance.
    c. physical dependence.
    d. psychoactive substance abuse.
    e. withdrawal syndrome.

    Answer: e   p. 583

16. Research evidence supports that 35 percent of people suffering from _____ also suffer from comorbid substance abuse disorders.
    a. schizophrenia
    b. depression
    c. bipolar disorder
    d. generalized anxiety disorder
    e. any of the above

    Answer: e   p. 584

17. Which kind of personality has research found to be associated with substance abuse?
    a. Addictive
    b. Antisocial
    c. Avoidant
    d. Dependent
    e. Oral

    Answer: b   p. 584

18. Antisocial personality disorder may predispose the individual to drug abuse
    a. because drug use is rewarding and not punishing.
    b. because it is found in those who are chronically underaroused.
    c. because it leads to a life of crime.
    d. because of a common underlying physiological mechanism.
    e. for reasons that are not clearly understood.

    Answer: e   p. 583

19. What subset of the general population is up to four times more likely to become alcohol dependent than the general population?
    a. Children of alcoholics
    b. Children born to mothers who drank during pregnancy
    c. Children who develop anxiety disorders
    d. Adolescents who develop borderline personality disorder
    e. Children who can be diagnosed with antisocial personality disorder

    Answer: a   p. 584

20. In applying the opponent-process model to addictive drugs, Process A corresponds to
    a. addiction.
    b. pleasure.
    c. tolerance.
    d. withdrawal.
    e. none of the above.

    Answer: b   p. 585

21. In applying the opponent-process model to addictive drugs, Process B corresponds to actual or fundamental
    a. addiction.
    b. pleasure.
    c. tolerance.
    d. withdrawal.
    e. none of the above.

    Answer: d   p. 585

22. According to the opponent-process model of addiction, Process B is the
    a. compensatory reaction stimulated by Process A.
    b. initial affective pleasure.
    c. compensatory reaction that augments Process A.
    d. compensatory reaction that stimulates Process C.
    e. process that diminishes over time.

    Answer: a   p. 585

23. According to the opponent-process model of addiction, which of the following is *not* associated with drug dependence?
    a. Affective contrast
    b. Affective dependence
    c. Affective pleasure
    d. Affective tolerance
    e. Affective withdrawal

    Answer: b   p. 585

24. The reinforcing properties of drugs in the brain are thought to involve the
    a. blood-brain barrier.
    b. hippocampus.
    c. nucleus accumbens.
    d. raphe nucleus.
    e. substantia nigra.

    Answer: c   p. 587

25. The brain contains chemicals that are morphine-like and are called
    a. hormones.
    b. neurotransmitters.
    c. endogenous opioids.
    d. heroin.
    e. morphine.

    Answer: c   p. 587

26. Endorphins are compounds produced in the body that are analogous to
    a. alcohol.
    b. cocaine.
    c. narcotics.
    d. sedative hypnotics.
    e. none of the above.

    Answer: c   p. 587

27. Opioids represent _____ whereas opiates represent _____.
    a. chemicals produced by the brain; narcotics
    b. narcotics; brain chemicals
    c. part of the limbic system; narcotics
    d. chemicals produced by the brain; part of the limbic system
    e. part of the limbic system; chemicals produced by the brain

    Answer: a   p. 587

28. Research suggests that _____ induce craving for a drug as well as play a role in triggering relapse.
    a. drug cues
    b. reward stimulus
    c. unconditioned stimulus
    d. conditioning
    e. punishment

    Answer: a   p. 588

29. Conditioned withdrawal
    a. may trigger relapse.
    b. is classically conditioned.
    c. can be elicited by drug cues.
    d. may occur in those no longer suffering withdrawal symptoms.
    e. all of the above.

    Answer: e   p. 588

30. Excluding cigarette smoking, the worst drug use problem in the United States is
    a. heroin abuse.
    b. cocaine abuse.
    c. alcoholism.
    d. coronary heart disease.
    e. high blood pressure.

    Answer: c   p. 589

31. Research shows that _____ are more likely to use and abuse alcohol.
    a. Caucasians
    b. African Americans
    c. Hispanics and Latinos
    d. Asians
    e. none of the above

    Answer: a   p. 589

32. What is the primary factor in determining the rate of absorption of alcohol?
    a. Concentration
    b. Amount drunk
    c. Mix with carbonation
    d. Amount of food in stomach
    e. Proportion of body fat

    Answer: a   p. 590

33. At higher levels, alcohol is associated with
    a. stimulant effects that may cause heart difficulties.
    b. hallucinogenic effects that may cause delusions.
    c. depressant effects that may impair sensory-motor functioning.
    d. depressant effects that may cause suicidal ideation.
    e. stimulant effects that may induce psychosis.

    Answer: c   p. 591

34. In general, alcohol acts as _____ on one's central nervous system.
    a. a stimulant
    b. a sedative
    c. a hallucinogen
    d. an opiate
    e. none of the above

    Answer: b   p. 592

35. Alcohol inhibits the GABA neurotransmitter system in the brain, and this is thought to account specifically for the _____ properties of the drug.
    a. stimulating
    b. mood-altering
    c. reinforcing
    d. depressant
    e. anxiety-relieving

    Answer: b   p. 592

36. Alcohol tolerance is characterized by all of these *except*
    a. behavioral tolerance.
    b. effective tolerance.
    c. metabolic tolerance.
    d. cellular tolerance.
    e. none of the above.

    Answer: b   p. 592

37. Delirium tremens, or D.T.s, occur in withdrawal from
    a. alcohol.
    b. cocaine.
    c. hallucinogens.
    d. narcotics.
    e. tobacco.

    Answer: a   p. 592

38. John, a new client, comes to see you because he has been drinking heavily for the last two years. He says that, as a result of his drinking, he has experienced many problems in his life. You decide to
    a. diagnose John with an alcohol withdrawal disorder.
    b. diagnose John with alcoholism.
    c. gather more information to determine if John meets diagnostic criteria for alcoholism.
    d. diagnose John with a substance abuse disorder.
    e. diagnose John with a substance dependence disorder.

    Answer: c   p. 593

39. If either of your parents are alcoholics, the chances of your also being an alcoholic are increased by
    a. 2.
    b. 4.
    c. 8.
    d. 10.
    e. 20.

    Answer: b   p. 594

40. All of the following have been found to be true of those at risk for alcoholism when compared to those not at risk *except*
    a. less body sway changes when under the influence of alcohol.
    b. less self-reported intoxication when under the influence of alcohol.
    c. subtle EEG abnormalities even before drinking age.
    d. low response to the effects of alcohol.
    e. all of the above are true.

    Answer: e   p. 595

41. Alcoholics report that alcohol helps them _____; however, observation of their behavior suggests that it makes them _____.
    a. have fun; enjoy things less
    b. make decisions; indecisive
    c. manage stress; more stressed
    d. perform difficult tasks; care less
    e. relax; depressed and anxious

    Answer: e   p. 596

42. Alcoholics who show a pattern of binge drinking rather than chronic drinking tend to
    a. have a strong genetic component.
    b. start drinking relatively early.
    c. experience feelings of anxiety and dependency.
    d. be male.
    e. all of the above.

    Answer: c   p. 597

43. If you were to assess a man who appears impulsive and novelty seeking, and he reports that his father is an alcoholic, his own alcohol abuse began in his teens, and he has difficulty abstaining, you would consider a diagnosis of
    a. negative effect alcoholism.
    b. developmentally limited alcoholism.
    c. Type 1 alcoholism.
    d. Type 2 alcoholism.
    e. milieu-independent alcoholism.

    Answer: d   p. 597

44. Generally, the first step in the treatment of alcoholism is
    a. detoxification.
    b. entering a 12-step program.
    c. entering the treatment phase.
    d. beginning drug therapy.
    e. none of the above.

    Answer: a   p. 598

45. The drug that inhibits the enzyme that aids in the metabolism of alcohol is called
    a. nalexone.
    b. naltrexone.
    c. disulfiram.
    d. methadone.
    e. lithium.

    Answer: c   p. 599

46. Recent findings that naltrexone can reduce relapse and craving in alcoholics suggests that _____ play a role in alcoholism.
    a. stimulants
    b. endogenous opioids
    c. opiates
    d. hallucinogens
    e. narcotics

    Answer: b   p. 599

47. About _____ of hospital admissions are alcohol related.
    a. 10 percent
    b. 20 percent
    c. 30 percent
    d. 40 percent
    e. 50 percent

    Answer: d   p. 600

48. Cocaine, amphetamine, and caffeine are all
    a. habit forming.
    b. hallucinogen.
    c. narcotic.
    d. stimulant.
    e. a and d.

    Answer: e   p. 600

49. Which of these has the strongest reinforcing properties?
    a. Alcohol
    b. Hallucinogens
    c. Narcotics
    d. Stimulants
    e. All of the above

    Answer: d   p. 600

50. A substance that research has shown is used almost universally, in suburbs, rural areas, and urban areas, regardless of race and socioeconomic status, is
    a. crack cocaine.
    b. methamphetamine.
    c. LSD.
    d. heroin.
    e. all of the above.

    Answer: b   p. 601

51. A 38-year-old very successful lawyer preparing for a big trial hasn't slept in three nights. His speech is rapid, his mood is somewhat irritable, and he is very restless. His wife brought him to the emergency room after he accused her in a threatening way of trying to make him lose the case. "He isn't himself," she says. He has no psychiatric history and no definite delusions. A physical exam reveals that his blood pressure and heart rate are elevated. Your first suspicion should be
    a. chronic narcotic use.
    b. schizophrenia.
    c. mania.
    d. alcohol withdrawal.
    e. chronic stimulant use.

    Answer: e   p. 602

52. The substance that is associated with the most medical problems is
    a. heroin.
    b. cocaine.
    c. marijuana.
    d. LSD.
    e. caffeine.

    Answer: b   p. 602

53. Cocaine intoxication shows itself primarily in changes in
    a. mood and emotional state.
    b. increased sexuality.
    c. heightened energy.
    d. cardiac rhythms.
    e. all of the above.

    Answer: e   p. 603

54. Psychostimulants, more than other drugs of abuse, rely primarily on their
    _____ to reinforce continued use.
    a. pharmacological effects on the dopamine system
    b. behavioral cues on the dopamine system
    c. operant effects
    d. classically conditioned effects.
    e. none of the above

    Answer: a   p. 604

55. Cocaine addiction is thought to occur as a result of
    a. dependency.
    b. neuroadaptation.
    c. behavioral cues.
    d. environmental cues.
    e. family reinforcers.

    Answer: b   p. 605

56. The triphasic abstinence pattern is characterized as
    a. crash → withdrawal → extinction.
    b. withdrawal → crash → extinction.
    c. extinction → crash → withdrawal.
    d. binge → crash → withdrawal.
    e. The steps are not thought to occur in any particular order.

    Answer: a   p. 606

57. Effective treatments for cocaine dependence should address which of the
    following?
    a. Conditioned physical responses
    b. Conditioned cravings
    c. Motivation to stay abstinent
    d. Depression in withdrawal phase
    e. All of the above

    Answer: e   p. 607

58. Opium comes from
    a. cactus.
    b. grass.
    c. morning glories.
    d. poppies.
    e. roses.

    Answer: d   p. 611

59. The most commonly abused opiate is
    a. heroin.
    b. morphine.
    c. methadone.
    d. opium.
    e. peyote.

    Answer: a   p. 612

60. Endorphins may be a product of evolution because they
    a. accentuate the effect of opium.
    b. alleviate boredom.
    c. preclude bipolar depression.
    d. predispose alcohol abuse.
    e. reduce pain.

    Answer: e   p. 613

61. Withdrawal from opiates resembles
    a. allergies.
    b. appendicitis.
    c. depression.
    d. influenza.
    e. anxiety.

    Answer: d   p. 615

62. The primary treatment for narcotic addiction is
    a. behavioral contingency management.
    b. cognitive restructuring.
    c. interpersonal therapy.
    d. psychodynamic therapy.
    e. pharmacological.

    Answer: e   p. 615

63. Substitution therapy for narcotics substitutes an abused opiate with one that is
    a. less expensive.
    b. more potent.
    c. more readily available.
    d. more socially acceptable.
    e. longer acting.

    Answer: e   p. 616

64. The most serious health consequences of opiate dependence result from
    a. the behavior of the addict.
    b. the pharmacological properties of the drug.
    c. neuroadaptation.
    d. the actual dependency.
    e. none of the above.

    Answer: a   p. 617

65. The text describes the social complications of narcotics as
    a. minimal.
    b. moderate.
    c. profound.
    d. variable.
    e. unknown.

    Answer: c   p. 617

66. One thing that differentiates the hallucinogens from other classes of drugs is their
    a. neurocognitive effects.
    b. ability to alter sensory perception and thoughts.
    c. addictive properties.
    d. pharmacological affects.
    e. behavioral components.

    Answer: b   p. 618

67. Which drug does *not* belong?
    a. Opium
    b. Psilocybin
    c. LSD
    d. Ecstacy
    e. PCP

    Answer: a   p. 618

68. Common to all hallucinogens is an effect on
    a. behavior.
    b. cognition.
    c. coordination.
    d. emotion.
    e. perception.

    Answer: e   p. 618

69. Which of these drug classes apparently *lacks* the reinforcing properties associated with dependence and addiction?
    a. Alcohol
    b. Hallucinogens
    c. Narcotics
    d. Stimulants
    e. None of the above

    Answer: b   p. 620

70. Episodes of panic occur among users of
    a. alcohol.
    b. hallucinogens.
    c. narcotics.
    d. stimulants.
    e. all of the above.

    Answer: b   p. 621

71. The most commonly used illicit substance is
    a. hallucinogens.
    b. opiates.
    c. stimulants.
    d. alcohol.
    e. marijuana.

    Answer: e   p. 622

72. Current opinion holds that prolonged marijuana use leads to
    a. tolerance.
    b. reverse tolerance.
    c. sensitization.
    d. desensitization.
    e. hyperappetite.

    Answer: a   p. 624

73. The medical and social complications of chronic marijuana use include all of these *except*
    a. impaired judgment.
    b. permanent cognitive impairment.
    c. amotivational syndrome.
    d. short-term memory impairment.
    e. bronchial conditions.

    Answer: b   p. 625

74. Tobacco was first smoked in
    a. Africa.
    b. America.
    c. Asia.
    d. Australia.
    e. Europe.

    Answer: b   p. 625

75. The psychoactive ingredient in tobacco is
    a. nicotine.
    b. tar.
    c. THC.
    d. opiate.
    e. fertilizers.

    Answer: a   p. 626

76. Tobacco is rated _____ on amount of intoxication and _____ as far as dependence.
    a. high; highest
    b. low; lowest
    c. highest; high
    d. low; highest
    e. low; low

    Answer: d   p. 627

77. Tobacco dependence resembles dependence on other drugs with respect to affective
    a. pleasure.
    b. tolerance.
    c. withdrawal.
    d. contrast.
    e. all of the above.

    Answer: e   p. 629

78. Cigarette smoking, as well as nicotine use in general, is more common in
_____ than in _____.
   a. the mentally ill; mentally healthy people
   b. children; adults
   c. women; mentally ill men
   d. severely mentally disabled; children
   e. none of the above

   Answer: e   p. 630

79. Which of these techniques is most effective in the long run for treating
tobacco dependence?
   a. Hypnosis
   b. Nicotine blockade
   c. Nicotine substitution
   d. Group counseling
   e. Behavioral therapy

   Answer: c   p. 630

80. The number one drug of dependence in the United States and the drug from
whose use deaths are the easiest to prevent is
   a. alcohol.
   b. hallucinogens.
   c. narcotics.
   d. stimulants.
   e. tobacco.

   Answer: e   p. 631

81. Smoking poses a hazard to health because it makes _____ more
likely.
   a. cancer
   b. coronary heart disease
   c. chronic pulmonary disease
   d. hypertension
   e. all of the above

   Answer: e   p. 630

82. Drugs whose primary effect is to depress the activity of the central nervous
system are called
   a. hallucinogens.
   b. opiates.
   c. barbiturates
   d. benzodiazepines.
   e. c and d

   Answer: e   p. 631

83. Which of the following interact with GABA?
    a. Alcohol
    b. Barbiturates
    c. Benzodiazepines
    d. All of the above
    e. b and c

    Answer: d   p. 631

84. The withdrawal syndrome associated with sedative cessation use is similar to that of
    a. alcohol.
    b. hallucinogens.
    c. narcotics.
    d. stimulants.
    e. all of the above.

    Answer: a   p. 633

85. The current position on whether the United States should legalize drugs is
    a. they should be legalized.
    b. they should not be legalized.
    c. evidence that legalization may work can be seen in other countries, but a definitive position remains unclear.
    d. they should be legalized but only for medical purposes.
    e. none of the above.

    Answer: c   p. 634

86. Which person should have the easier time stopping his or her drug abuse?
    a. Someone using a drug in a variety of situations
    b. Someone using a drug that is hard to obtain
    c. Someone using a drug with a long B process
    d. Someone using a drug with narcotic properties
    e. None of the above

    Answer: b   p. 635

CHAPTER 15 | Social and Legal Perspectives

1. Some people in the general public view the symptoms of mental illness as willful and offensive. The effect of these views on those with mental illness is that they are
   a. made more ill.
   b. receive less attention.
   c. stigmatized.
   d. able to get better services.
   e. none of the above.

   Answer: c   p. 640

2. The biggest cost to the family of someone suffering from mental illness is
   a. monetary.
   b. emotional.
   c. reproductive.
   d. stigma.
   e. increased risk for developing a mental illness.

   Answer: b   p. 642

3. That the criminal justice system is carrying a large percentage of the cost to society of mental illness is called
   a. deinstitutionalization.
   b. stigmatization.
   c. managed care.
   d. criminalization.
   e. none of the above.

   Answer: d   p. 643

4. During the 1960s and 1970s a process called _____ was likely largely impacted by _____.
   a. criminalization; managed care
   b. deinstitutionalization; psychotropic medications
   c. stigmatization; psychotropic medications
   d. criminalization; stigmatization
   e. deinstitutionalization; stigmatization

   Answer: b   p. 645

5. As a result of _____, the patient's bill of rights was constructed.
   a. stigmatization
   b. criminalization
   c. patient and family activism
   d. psychosocialization of society
   e. psychotropic medications

   Answer: c   p. 647
   c

6. Commitment to a psychiatric facility without giving consent is called
   a. involuntary commitment.
   b. stigmatization.
   c. civil commitment.
   d. deinstitutionalization.
   e. a and c.

   Answer: e   p. 649

7. What of the following bests describes the "thank you" test? Involuntary commitment is justified if
   a. friends and family members are grateful.
   b. society as a whole is grateful.
   c. the person, when recovered, is grateful.
   d. the person, when recovered, is not grateful.
   e. the hospital staff feels that the person will be grateful after recovery.

   Answer: c   p. 650

8. Commitment procedures require all of the following elements *except*
   a. dangerousness to self or others.
   b. the presence of a mental disorder.
   c. grave disability.
   d. a criminal act.
   e. none of the above.

   Answer: d   p. 651

9. According to the American Psychiatric Association, a *severe* mental disorder is defined as an illness, disease, or organic brain disorder that substantially impairs
   a. thought, perception of reality, emotional process, or judgment.
   b. behavior as manifested by recent disturbed behavior.
   c. ability to provide for one's basic needs.
   d. life choices.
   e. all of the above.

   Answer: a   p. 652

10. The most common justification for involuntary commitment is that the individual
    a. is dangerous to self or others.
    b. has impaired judgment.
    c. needs treatment.
    d. shows psychological disability.
    e. all of the above.

    Answer: a   p. 652

11. Some mentally ill homeless people, by the fact of their homelessness, may fit which of the following commitment criteria?
    a. Dangerous to self
    b. Dangerous to others
    c. Gravely disabled
    d. Needing treatment
    e. Any of the above

    Answer: c   p. 653

12. The legal problem in committing someone because she or he might be dangerous is
    a. that most people who might hurt themselves or others usually don't.
    b. that the prediction of violence is less than certain.
    c. that people have the right to be dangerous.
    d. that people should not be punished prior to a crime.
    e. none of the above.

    Answer: d   p. 653

13. The scientific problem in committing someone because he or she might be dangerous is
    a. that most people who might hurt themselves or others usually don't.
    b. that the prediction of violence is less than certain.
    c. that people have the right to be dangerous.
    d. that people should not be punished prior to a crime.
    e. a and b.

    Answer: b   p. 653

14. Operation Baxstrom refers to the release of patients from prison hospitals because
    a. new treatments were available outside.
    b. their sentence had expired.
    c. there was no room for them.
    d. they had been cured.
    e. they were sorry for their crime.

    Answer: b   p. 653

15. Recent research shows that future violence in male patients can be predicted with _____ accuracy.
    a. perfect
    b. high
    c. better than chance
    d. no
    e. Research is contradictory.

    Answer: c   p. 653

16. Due process refers to
    a. bureaucratic red tape.
    b. civil rights.
    c. open housing legislation.
    d. rights and privileges accorded to defendants.
    e. the right to vote.

    Answer: d   p. 654

17. Courts have ruled that mental patients cannot be denied
    a. due process.
    b. effective treatment.
    c. equal opportunity.
    d. free education.
    e. the right to vote.

    Answer: a   p. 654

18. Which is the most stringent standard of legal proof?
    a. Beyond a reasonable doubt
    b. Clear and convincing proof
    c. Preponderance of evidence
    d. Compelling proof
    e. They are all equivalent.

    Answer: a   p. 654

19. Which is the *least* stringent standard of legal proof?
    a. Beyond a reasonable doubt
    b. Clear and convincing proof
    c. Preponderance of evidence
    d. Incontrovertible proof
    e. They are all equivalent.

    Answer: c   p. 654

20. In 1979 the Supreme Court ruled which standard of legal proof should be used to decide involuntary commitment?
    a. Beyond a reasonable doubt
    b. Clear and convincing proof
    c. Preponderance of evidence
    d. Incontrovertible proof
    e. None of the above

    Answer: b   p. 654

21. Several court decisions have ruled that people involuntarily committed are entitled to
    a. second opinions.
    b. treatment.
    c. visitors.
    d. weekend passes.
    e. all of the above.

    Answer: b   p. 655

22. An unfortunate reaction to the growing rights of committed patients is that they have been
    a. discharged from hospitals into substandard housing.
    b. more likely to be given experimental drugs.
    c. ostracized by lawyers.
    d. sued by their psychologists.
    e. all of the above.

    Answer: a   p. 656

23. A positive reaction to the release of mental patients is the
    a. creation of a governmental agency to protect the rights of mental patients.
    b. development of more effective outpatient therapies.
    c. growth of the work force.
    d. improvement of conditions within hospitals.
    e. patients' rights movement.

    Answer: e   p. 656

24. According to the text, mental patients are best off when treated in
    a. board-and-care homes.
    b. community-based programs.
    c. homes of their families.
    d. hospitals.
    e. none of the above.

    Answer: b   p. 656

25. Many critics of psychiatry, such as Thomas Szasz, oppose
    a. involuntary commitment.
    b. involuntary treatment.
    c. commitment of any kind.
    d. all of the above.
    e. none of the above.

    Answer: d   p. 657

26. All versions of the insanity defense require that the person be irrational
    a. after the crime was committed.
    b. before the crime was committed.
    c. when the crime was committed.
    d. when the trial is held.
    e. all of the above.

    Answer: c   p. 657

27. The insanity plea is used in about 1 of _____ homicide cases that go to trial.
    a. 2
    b. 10
    c. 100
    d. 400
    e. 1,000

    Answer: d   p. 660

28. People judged incompetent to stand trial are believed to be
    a. psychologically absent.
    b. unable to understand the proceedings against them.
    c. unable to participate in their own defense.
    d. suffering from a mental disease.
    e. all of the above.

    Answer: e   p. 657

29. Defendants are found incompetent to stand trial _____ not guilty
   by reason of insanity.
   a. much more frequently than
   b. somewhat more frequently than
   c. with equal frequently as
   d. somewhat less frequently than
   e. much less frequently than

   Answer: a   p. 657

30. Current court rulings hold that people judged incompetent to stand trial
   a. can be held indefinitely if they are guilty.
   b. can be held indefinitely if they are improving.
   c. can be held indefinitely if they are not improving.
   d. cannot be held indefinitely.
   e. must be tried eventually, regardless of competence.

   Answer: d   p. 658 _

31. According to the text, the insanity plea is needed to
   a. allow society to punish people who have committed no crime.
   b. maintain the assumption that behavior reflects free will.
   c. protect victims.
   d. reflect the fact that behavior is determined.
   e. streamline trials.

   Answer: b   p. 660

32. Which of these might be described as a "right-wrong" test?
   a. ALI
   b. Durham
   c. GBMI
   d. M'Naghten
   e. "Thank you"

   Answer: d   p. 662

33. Which of these tests is the most narrow?
   a. ALI
   b. Durham
   c. GBMI
   d. M'Naghten
   e. "Thank you"

   Answer: d   p. 662

34. Which of these is a "product of mental diseases" test?
    a. ALI
    b. Durham
    c. GBMI
    d. M'Naghten
    e. "Thank you"

    Answer: b   p. 663

35. Which of these tests is the most broad?
    a. ALI
    b. Durham
    c. GBMI
    d. M'Naghten
    e. "Thank you"

    Answer: b   p. 663

36. Which of these is an "appreciate and conform" test?
    a. ALI
    b. Durham
    c. GBMI
    d. M'Naghten
    e. "Thank you"

    Answer: a   p. 664

37. Which of these tests is little used today?
    a. ALI
    b. Durham
    c. M'Naghten
    d. GBMI
    e. "Thank you"

    Answer: b   p. 665

38. ALI is to GBMI as
    a. appreciate is to conform.
    b. new is to old.
    c. not guilty is to guilty.
    d. mental disease is to right and wrong.
    e. intent is to act.

    Answer: c   p. 666

39. A judgement of "guilty but mentally ill" sends a person
    a. to a mental institution.
    b. to prison.
    c. home.
    d. to a rehabilitation center.
    e. a or b.

    Answer: a   p. 667

40. The text criticizes the "guilty but mentally ill" verdict because it is
    a. contradictory.
    b. harsh.
    c. lenient.
    d. used too frequently.
    e. used too infrequently.

    Answer: a   p. 667

41. The phenomenon of amnesia for traumatic events associated with distressing emotions is called
    a. delayed discovery.
    b. the unconscious.
    c. repressed memory.
    d. suppressed memory.
    e. recovered memory.

    Answer: c   p. 668

42. Which of the following is *not* a problem inherent in the issue of recovered memories and the law?
    a. Determining whether the remembered event occurred at all
    b. Statutes of limitations
    c. Delayed discovery doctrine
    d. Veracity of the specific content of the memory
    e. Feelings of authenticity

    Answer: c   p. 669

43. Of concern to clinicians when discussing the abuse of clients is
    a. sexual relations between therapists and clients.
    b. stigmatization.
    c. deinstitutionalization.
    d. the use of pharmaceuticals.
    e. none of the above.

    Answer: a   p. 671

44. Abusive use of the principles and tenets of abnormal psychology in political and social realms occurs
    a. consciously.
    b. in the Soviet Union.
    c. in the United States.
    d. unconsciously.
    e. all of the above.

    Answer: e   p. 672

45. Abusive use of the principles and tenets of abnormal psychology by the state is caused by _____, and in society by _____.
    a. anger; anger
    b. anger; fear
    c. fear; anger
    d. fear; fear
    e. all of the above

    Answer: d   p. 672

CHAPTER 16 | Future Directions

1. While murder is not a diagnostic category in the DSM-IV, future directions may begin to look at
   a. abnormal behavior that occurs prior to any display of violent or murderous behavior.
   b. the treatment of choice for murders.
   c. a redefinition of the causes of murders.
   d. the right of a murderer to treatment.
   e. the analysis of school behavior as a predictor of murder.

   Answer: a   p. 680

2. Childhood factors that are a sign of the times and may shed light on the increase in violent behavior in children are
   a. impulsivity and present-focused thinking.
   b. victimology and the need for instant gratification.
   c. increased bullying and anger episodes.
   d. newly developed psychological factors and diagnoses.
   e. a and b

   Answer: e   p. 683

3. When compared to those convicted for murder, members of control groups show
   a. increased prefrontal activity.
   b. less problems with temper control.
   c. more impulsivity.
   d. a more-detailed present-minded focus.
   e. more limbic system activity.

   Answer: a   p. 683

4. In the *Consumer Reports* research, results showed
   a. that in general, treatment is effective.
   b. that certain treatment modalities (i.e., cognitive-behavioral) were more effective.
   c. that length of treatment was not important in treatment effectiveness.
   d. that efficacy was not related to effectiveness.
   e. none of the above.

   Answer: a   p. 685

5. In the *Consumer Reports* research, results showed
   a. that in general, treatment is ineffective.
   b. that certain treatment modalities (i.e., cognitive-behavioral) were more effective.
   c. that length of treatment was important in treatment effectiveness.
   d. that efficacy was not related to effectiveness.
   e. none of the above.

   Answer: c   p. 685

6. In the *Consumer Reports* research, results suggested that short-term therapy was _____ than long-term therapy.
   a. less effective
   b. less efficacious
   c. more effective
   d. more efficacious
   e. a and b

   Answer: a   p. 685

7. Evidence suggests that _____ is large in any studies on psychotherapy.
   a. the effect size estimate
   b. the placebo effect
   c. the number of subjects
   d. the error
   e. none of the above

   Answer: b   p. 687

8. Instilling hope and building buffering strengths are examples of
   a. placebo effects.
   b. tactics.
   c. fixed duration techniques.
   d. deep strategies.
   e. active strategies.

   Answer: d   p. 687

9. One of the biggest changes in psychotherapy in the last few decades is the
   a. movement from short-term therapies to long-term therapies.
   b. application of research to clinical practice.
   c. development of a patients' bill of rights.
   d. refinement of the insanity plea.
   e. movement from point of service to managed care.

   Answer: e   p. 688

10. The downside of managed care in psychotherapy is
    a. the widening gulf between what therapists think they should do and what they are allowed to do.
    b. the widening of the gulf between good science and good practice.
    c. its being eliminated as a viable treatment option.
    d. more people seeking treatment with fewer therapists to serve them.
    e. a and b

    Answer: e   p. 689

11. In recent years there has been a movement toward _____ instead of
    _____.
    a. prevention; treatment
    b. point of service treatment; managed care
    c. long-term therapies; short-term therapies
    d. prevention; managed care
    e. point of service treatment; intervention strategies

    Answer: a   p. 689

12. One of the critical factors in preventing depression is the
    a. severity of depression in family members.
    b. age at which the prevention occurs.
    c. use of medications in at-risk populations.
    d. use of the coping cat.
    e. use of the coping koala.

    Answer: b   p. 690

13. An effect method for preventing anxiety in at-risk populations is
    a. teaching cognitive and problem-solving skills.
    b. using psychoanalytic techniques to address unresolved conflicts.
    c. using medications.
    d. refraining from using booster sessions.
    e. none of the above.

    Answer: a   p. 690

14. The coping cat is an example of a manualized
    a. prevention program for children.
    b. treatment program for children.
    c. prevention program for adults.
    d. treatment program for adults.
    e. none of the above.

    Answer: b   p. 690

15. The coping koala is an example of a manualized
    a. prevention program for children.
    b. treatment program for children.
    c. prevention program for adults.
    d. treatment program for adults.
    e. none of the above.

    Answer: a   p. 690

16. Both the coping koala and the coping cat are
    a. long-term treatment programs for children.
    b. short-term behavioral treatments for children.
    c. cognitive and problem-solving skills manuals for children.
    d. children's fantasy books.
    e. parent training manuals.

    Answer: c   p. 691

17. Which of the following are the two mental health epidemics in the United States today?
    a. Anxiety and schizophrenia
    b. Depression and perihelia
    c. Depression and substance abuse
    d. Aggression and violence
    e. Depression, and aggression and violence

    Answer: e   p. 690

18. Are prevention programs effective at reducing aggression and violence?
    a. No.
    b. Yes.
    c. Only when administered to middle-class Caucasian children.
    d. Only when administered to males.
    e. None of the above.

    Answer: b   p. 692

19. A current movement in psychology is away from the _____ and toward _____.
    a. disease model; building human strengths
    b. criminal model; the disease model
    c. disease model; the criminal model
    d. criminal model; building human strengths
    e. criminal model; positive psychotherapy

    Answer: a   p. 692

20. Positive psychology focuses on
    a. building human strengths.
    b. criminalizing psychological illness.
    c. ensuring future use of the disease model.
    d. detailing new directions in treatment rather than prevention.
    e. a and d.

    Answer: a   p. 693